Frederick A. Ober

The Knockabout Club in the Everglades

The Adventures of the Club in exploring Lake Okechobee

Frederick A. Ober

The Knockabout Club in the Everglades
The Adventures of the Club in exploring Lake Okechobee

ISBN/EAN: 9783743308077

Manufactured in Europe, USA, Canada, Australia, Japa

Cover: Foto ©ninafisch / pixelio.de

Manufactured and distributed by brebook publishing software (www.brebook.com)

Frederick A. Ober

The Knockabout Club in the Everglades

THE KNOCKABOUT CLUB

IN THE EVERGLADES.

THE
KNOCKABOUT CLUB.

NOW PUBLISHED.

KNOCKABOUT CLUB IN THE WOODS.

KNOCKABOUT CLUB ALONGSHORE.

KNOCKABOUT CLUB IN THE TROPICS.

By C. A. STEPHENS,
AUTHOR OF "THE YOUNG MOOSE-HUNTERS," "CAMPING OUT," ETC.

KNOCKABOUT CLUB IN THE EVERGLADES.

By F. A. OBER,
AUTHOR OF "TRAVELS IN MEXICO," ETC.

IN THE EVERGLADES.

FULLY ILLUSTRATED

BOSTON
ESTES AND LAURIAT

CONTENTS.

CHAPTER
- I. ON BOARD THE "WANDERING WIND"
- II. THE GREAT MOSQUITO LAGOON
- III. AMONG THE LIVE-OAKERS
- IV. POTTERY AND PANTHERS
- V. A HUNT FOR TURTLE-EGGS
- VI. DOWN THE INDIAN RIVER
- VII. A BEAR-HUNT ON THE BEACH
- VIII. GOOD INDIANS AND BAD WHITE MEN
- IX. TEN DAYS WITH THE SEMINOLES
- X. LAKE OKECHOBEE
- XI. MORE ABOUT LAKE OKECHOBEE
- XII. INDIAN TRADITIONS AND FOLK-LORE
- XIII. SOMETHING ABOUT CAMPING OUT
- XIV. A TURKEY-HUNT IN THE PINY WOODS
- XV. HERONS AND ALLIGATORS
- XVI. DOWN THE OCKLAWAHA

ILLUSTRATIONS.

	PAGE
In the Everglades . . . . . *Frontispiece*	
The "Wandering Wind" bound out	13
Florida Coast	19
Lighthouse on the Coast	23
Scissor-Bills fishing	25
Fishing on the Florida Coast	27
An Episode of the Seminole War	35
"Numerous channels running off east and west"	39
The House on the Lagoon	43
The Naturalist in Florida	47
"A panther crept stealthily up"	51
Fishing for the Hammer-Fish	55
"Seizing a flipper and laying hold beneath the upper shell"	58
Phosphorescence at Sea	59
Tiger Tail	65
A Little Bay back of Oleander Point	67
The Great Colony of Pelicans	71
"A black paw reached up and grasped the rail"	75
"Birds that hovered in clouds above the bar"	79
Turtle on the Beach	81
Hunted by the Bear	83
"Toting" the Bear	87
"As soon as the anchor dropped we all turned in"	91
An Okechobee Indian	93
The Murderers' Cabin	95
The Camp in the Pine Woods	97
"Lang was a shrewd German"	100
Osceola, Chief of the Seminoles	103

	PAGE
"The desperate leaps of our frightened horses"	104
"His plantation was a mile away, in the cypress hammock"	105
"The next day the performance began"	109
"The gloom of the cypress"	113
"It was a desperate situation"	117
"Impenetrable swamp and gloomy forest"	119
On the St. John's	123
Van Buster	126
Flats and Prairies of the St. John's	130
Herons	135
"Soon the river resumed its crooked course"	139
The Camp on the Island	143
A Mounted Warrior	153
Indian Scalp-Dance	157
Indian Burial-Place	161
An Incident in Indian Warfare	165
Death of King Philip	169
Burial of De Soto	173
A Curious Floating Island	177
An Unpleasant Neighbor	181
One of the Doctor's Finds	184
The Home of the Heron	187
Herons and Alligators	193
Green Heron	197
"I was astride the tail, in the stern of the boat"	200
"Two brawny men soon after entered"	209
A "Walking-Stick"	212

THE
KNOCKABOUT CLUB IN THE EVERGLADES.

CHAPTER I.

ON BOARD THE "WANDERING WIND."

THE MATE ON DECK.

THE "Wandering Wind" was a handsome schooner, of about two hundred tons; and the second trip she ever made was perhaps the most famous of all, before and after, because it was on this voyage she carried the party whose adventures are to be herewith described. The "party" proper consisted of two individuals. Their fares were paid to Mosquito Inlet, coast of Florida; and their luggage and merchandise — a ton's weight or more — were stowed away in the hold. It was a cold December day on which they left Boston and sailed out of its harbor. That night their vessel managed to double Cape Cod; but the greater part of the following week was passed in various harbors on the south coast of the cape, either wind-bound or rolling at the mercy of the heavy seas.

Even after ten days had passed, they were no farther along than the harbor of Newport; but after that they struck the right wind on the quarter, and put to sea in good earnest. They made such good time that the "Wandering Wind" was driven in shore near Frying-Pan Shoals by a gale that came along out of season, and narrowly escaped the fate of a government cruiser which foundered almost before their very eyes. The mate said that he thought they "might as well visit every harbor on the Atlantic coast, and done with it;" and if they ever got to Florida, they might thank their lucky stars. But they did reach their destination three weeks from the day they last sighted the Massachusetts coast, though after more misery and sea-sickness than they had ever imagined one life could hold.

The mate of the "Wandering Wind" was the only man on board not gloomy and morose; and he, to cheer them in their "sea-sickest days," as he expressed it, would spin yarns that would tax their credulity and excite their amazement. He had travelled sailor-fashion all over the world; but the place of all places to him seemed to be San Francisco.

"You were n't never there, were ye? Well, I tell you it 's a big city. Cost me fifty dollars a day when I went there fust. Cheap place to live in? Of course it is, — cheapest in the world. You can get a square meal for ten cents, all you want to eat, — taters, biled dinner, corned beef; but I had money them days, and went in for a good time.

"And them Chinymen! They 're snug, them Chinymen; don't spend a dollar a week. They 're great on Mexican dollars; bag up all they can get, and send 'em home to Chiny.

"I saw an old Chinyman once, in Singapore, goin' along the streets with a big bag of 'em on his shoulders. He was then in front of the 'Caledonia,' a kind of hotel, in which was about one hundred and fifty English men-o'-war's men; an' they was just a-carryin' on, — they was, you know; an' one on 'em went out, and took his knife and slashed it across the stern of that bag of dollars, and then all them sailors went for 'em. You ought to have seen 'em scrabble! And there was the old Chinyman down on all-fours, and goin' this way

THE "WANDERING WIND" BOUND OUT.

and that, and spittin' and swearin', and they a-passin' him from one to t' other! I'll bet he did n't save five dollars out of the whole lot.

"Then he went and got a lot more Chinymen, and they all come up with clubs and knives, and tackled them sailors. But, bless you! it wa'n't no use at all.

"Them man-o'-war's men would chase 'em, and git 'em by their pig-tails, and cut 'em off chock-a-block. And you ought to see the way them Chinymen run! You see, they wear these wooden shoes, and there ain't nothin' to keep 'em on but a peg that sticks right up between their toes; and them fellers would just travel, and them shoes would fly way up over their heads, and they would n't haul up a bit, but just kept right on till they outsailed the Jacks.

"After that they had a regular riot, the man-o'-war's men and the Chiny fellers and a lot of Rooshun sailors; and they was a-draggin' Chinymen out of the canal for three days afterwards. Oh, they was a-carryin' on awfully!

"But I did n't tell you about my v'yage in the 'Orient.' Oh, that was a trip worth taking! We sailors shipped at ten o'clock one night, and at 'leven a side-wheeler hooked on to us, and did n't let go till it had towed us outside Sandy Hook. Then we set sail for Africa; had a good v'yage; got there all right. But we was on a bad business; for it wa'n't nothin' more nor less than nigger-stealin', — for that was before the war, when the South took all the black men we could smuggle in.

"There was two English men-o'-war steamers off the mouth of the Congo; but we give them the slip in the night, and passed up the river right between 'em.

"It was all right so far; and we 'd got our cargo landed and all our water aboard and about twenty niggers, when we heard there was a couple of barges comin' up the river; for they used to reconnoitre every few weeks. I tell you we just hustled them niggers ashore. It did n't make no difference to them whether they had irons on or not; they could swim just as well; and so we chucked 'em overboard, and they paddled ashore just like dogs. Of course the barges had hove in sight by that time, and they see some of the niggers runnin' for the woods.

"Well, they put a crew aboard, and sent down the river for the steamer, and that steamer come up and hitched on to us and towed us out of the river and down the coast for two days and nights, and all that time the cap'n of the steamer was closeted with the cap'n of our vessel and tryin' to get him to give up the ship's papers.

"Finally, our cap'n come up, and told us that he had been obliged to give up the papers, and said he thought the best thing we could do was to haul down the flag and give ourselves up, and perhaps we could have the long-boat, and so might reach a settlement and get clear.

"As long as the American flag was flyin' over us the English cap'n did n't dare to overhaul us; but if he could get one of our men to haul it down, then he would take possession and have the ship as a prize.

"Our mate he was an old man, but full of pluck; and when the cap'n had gone below, he said to us: 'Well, men, how is it? Are we goin' to haul down the flag?'

"And we vowed we would n't; for we knew just how the Britisher would serve us. Then the old mate went below, and when he come up he had two revolvers in his belt.

"'Now,' said he, 'the first man that gits into them ratlines to haul down that flag gits a bullet in his head!'

"Next day, the English officer come aboard, and asked us if we 'd haul down the flag. The first mate said, 'No!'

"'Don't you think,' said Johnny Bull, 'that I can send a man up there and haul it down?'

"'Yes, you can; but you won't,' said the mate. 'When you do that you overstep your authority; the commodore is the only man can do that, and he does it at his own risk.' And says he, 'The first man that tries that on will die, as sure as I 've got twelve charges in these revolvers!'

"Johnny Bull glared at him, and then he said, 'I'll string you up to the yard-arm as soon as I do get possession!'

"'All right! when you do, you can,' said the mate. Well, they kept us there seven months, right between two men-o'-war, until our man-o'-war come down; then we were delivered up to her.

"We were struck by lightnin', I remember, while we was layin' there. The bolt come down and rattled round our chain-box till the chains were twisted into all the kinds of kinks and half-hitches you ever see. I saw it travel for'ard, a great ball of fire as big as my head, and then come back and rattle round in that chain-box again, and carry on like a train of cars on a dock. Then all at once it stopped, and I s'pose it went out the hawse-hole into the water.

"And there were them Jack-o-lanterns, will-o'-the-wisps, or Saint Elmo's fires, or whatever-you-call-'em; we used to have them almost every night. I've seen 'em at the end of a yard-arm, and have crawled out to within six feet of 'em, when they'd disappear; I could n't ever reach one.

"When the commodore of our man-o'-war was overhaulin' us, the English cap'n he would come aboard, and watch all proceedin's; and his sailors would steal all they could git their hands on. Our mate he saw all there was goin' on, but he did n't say nothin' till the cap'n had stepped aboard his gig; then the mate told the commodore he did n't want them Englishmen carryin' off all our stores. The commodore says to the cap'n, says he, 'The mate says your men are carryin' off his stores.' Well, they had the stern of the gig stowed full of canned meats and such. The English cap'n he turned red and glared at the mate, but did n't say nothin'; but next mornin' he strung them sailors up and whipped 'em so two of 'em died. We could hear every blow of the cat. That was at eight o'clock, and at 'leven two of 'em was carried ashore and buried.

"Well, young men, they sent us home, put a prize crew aboard, and sailed for New York. When they got there, they chucked us into jail and ironed us with them same nigger manacles; and when we went from the jail to the court-room, every nigger in New York was a-follerin' us, hootin' and yellin'.

"When I got into court I felt kind of blue, and thinks I, this 'ere is carryin' on awful; and when I see them big-wigs a-writin' and scribblin' 'round, I thought 't was all up with us.

"But a feller behind touched me on the arm and says, says he, 'Don't git down in the mouth, hearty; it's goin' to be all right with you fellers;' and sure enough, so 't was, after a few days. They marched us back to jail; and next day old Gomez, a Portuguese, who owned most of the 'Orient,' come down and told the keeper to let us have anything we wanted from outside, — wine, cigars, or anything. And I tell you, we kept our skins full. In a few days we were all out on bail. The old keeper, he says, when he saw us goin', 'I'm mighty sorry you're goin', boys, mighty sorry!'

"We stayed there on bail a month, a-gettin' our ten dollars a day, — to keep us there, you know; for they was afraid we'd go off, and they'd lose our bail money. But there wa'n't no fear of that; for all we had to do was to go down from the hotel to the court-house at ten o'clock, report, make a round turn up through the park and back again to the hotel.

"Oh, they was gay times, and we all carried on awfully!

"After they had cleared us from the charge of nigger-stealin' I shipped aboard a government vessel that supplied the light-houses along the coast. We had a good cap'n, Cap'n Colman, but he was the fussiest old chap you ever see. Whenever he spied a sail anywhere he always gave chase, even if 't was goin' in another direction from what we was.

"One day, after chasin' a brig for nigh half a day, he finally come up with her, and propounded his long string of questions that he always asked. Then, as usual, he leaned over the rail, and told 'em that his vessel was the 'Cynthia;' been to Galveston, supplyin' light-houses along the coast, and now goin' back to New Bedford. Then he told 'em his name was Colman, — C-o-l-m-a-n, Colman. The other cap'n listened patiently, and then bellowed back, 'What do I care for all that, you old fool!' Cap'n Colman was silent a minute; then he turned to the man at the wheel and said, 'Keep her off, Timothy, keep her off; he's a brute!'"

Thus did the mate spin out his yarns, day after day; but with these as a sample of his sailor lingo, we will now let him drop out of sight.

FLORIDA COAST.

As soon as land was announced all thought of other things faded out of mind. It was on the first day of January that they saw the Florida coast, — a long, low, hazy line to westward. At night they could see the trees on shore, and just at sunset caught a glimpse of two vessels at anchor inside the inlet, or break in the beach, through which they must sail to the great lagoons beyond.

The captain of the "Wandering Wind" dropped anchor till morning, as the breeze had died away and the inlet was too narrow to be entered at night.

CHAPTER II.

THE GREAT MOSQUITO LAGOON.

AT daylight, next morning, the schooner drifted down opposite the inlet, and a pilot-boat came out to her. Then she was headed for the breakers, which rolled up the sands on either hand, and burst upon the wreck of a vessel almost in mid-channel. A steamer came out,—the "George M. Bird,"— and the schooner was towed in through the narrow, tortuous, and dangerous channel, and tied up to a wharf on the left-hand bank of the lagoon.

They were, at last, inside the famous Mosquito Inlet, about sixty miles south of the historic old city of St. Augustine. From the outside the inlet presents only a long line of foaming breakers, with no entrance visible; and it requires pilots of nerve and experience to navigate its devious channel, which sometimes shifts about with every gale that blows. Any vessel drawing more than eight feet of water would have hard luck in entering, and probably strike and go to pieces. But the "Wandering Wind" had been here before, and she was loaded light with hay; hence we find her passengers safely landed on the shore of the great Mosquito Lagoon.

The collector of the port, at the time of the arrival of the expedition in Florida waters, was Major Alden, a lineal descendant of the redoubtable John Alden; and he received the boys with all the hospitality to be expected of one of this historic name. His house was perched upon a shelly bluff overlooking the inlet, the Mosquito Lagoon and Halifax River coming down from the north. There were but two houses between the Major's and the inlet, two miles away, and his wharf was the best in the lagoon.

Half a mile from his house, across a sunken plain covered with scrub-palmetto and live-oak forest, was the sea-beach, which ran southward many miles without a break. Here the boys went in bathing on the fourth day of January, finding the water excellent, and not cold at all. But a big sea-wave came roaring up and washed off their clothes, which they with difficulty rescued, and they thought they could see the fins of several sharks cutting the water amidst the foam.

Sitting on the broad piazza of the Major's house most of the time during the first week in January, the boys arranged the details of the exploration they had undertaken.

North of them lay the inlet with its foaming bar, two miles away, hidden by a palm-fringed headland; westward from that could be seen the lower end of Halifax Lagoon, and the peninsula between this salt river and the ocean, stretching northward. West was a broad expanse of marsh, intersected by numerous creeks, dotted with mangroves and palmettos, and bounded by a horizon of pines. Nearly southwest across the marsh lay New Smyrna, showing only three houses of its small hamlet. Stretching southward was a vast waste of scrub-land and pine-barren, with a line of mangroves fringing the Hillsborough River. It was very pleasant to sit there and watch the scene spread out below them, — the peaceful river, over which, every morning, flew flocks of wild ducks and fish-crows, with great blue herons fishing on its margin, and flocks of terns, plover, and curlew skimming its surface. The curious shear-water, or scissor-bills, enlivened the scene by his odd flight at times, and the willet and kill-deer plover by their tell-tale cries.

LIGHTHOUSE ON THE COAST.

A prominent point in sight between them and the inlet was Massacre Bluff, where a crew of shipwrecked sailors were killed by Seminole Indians forty years ago.

But what was this expedition, thus undertaken, and the members of which we find sunning themselves upon the Major's piazza?

In brief, these two boys had undertaken to explore a portion of Florida that was absolutely unknown at that time. The leader

SCISSOR-BILLS FISHING.

had already been once to Florida, but the younger member was now taking his first long journey from home.

As each one bore equal share in the arduous labor, each had his adventures, and each took his turn in writing the journal of which this story is the outgrowth and faithful record, no special prominence will be given to any member of the expedition.

It is the expressed wish of the participants in this exploration that their individuality be merged into one, and that the story be told as though written by one person. In this manner all heartburnings will be avoided, no one will feel slighted, and the reader's undivided attention may be given to the narrative.

But each boy (or *young man*, if you prefer) had his individual preferences, manifested by the attention he paid to certain subjects. One of them was as eager for new birds as Audubon; the other was equally interested in the history and antiquities of Florida. Both were united in the desire to co-operate for some end, and wished the result of their exploration to be good in every way.

To further this they had had built, in Massachusetts, two flat-bottomed boats, one twenty-one feet long and seven broad, and the other twelve feet long, to act as a sort of tender to the larger. They were made of white pine and very light, yet capable of carrying heavy loads. These they launched, soon after their arrival in the lagoon, and loaded with their goods as fast as they could be removed from the hold of the "Wandering Wind." A more miscellaneous lot of material had never, probably, been brought to Florida's shores; for it included dry-goods, groceries, arms, ammunition, arsenic (for preserving birdskins), beads and jewelry (for trade with the Indians), and, in fact, everything necessary for subsistence in a wild and thinly settled country. When loaded with their goods, the large boat was brought nearly to the water's edge; and then it was discovered that everything must be taken out, and a centre-board be put in, to improve her sailing qualities.

This took several days; so the tent (which they had brought with them) was pitched on shore, and all the goods stored under it, and a watch kept over it, night and day, to keep away the half-wild hogs that roamed the beach.

Little by little the plan was unfolded to the Major, and his approval gained. When he learned that the young men had as their destination the great Lake Okeechobee, and that they intended to explore it fully before their return, he was nearly wild to accompany them. But this he could not do; so he lent his

FISHING ON THE FLORIDA COAST.

aid and experience to them in providing for the long and dangerous journey.

He was open-hearted and generous in his dealings with them, and determined that they should succeed; hence he kept them with him until fully equipped for their long voyage, and it was nearly two weeks before they took their departure.

The day before they left him, he came over from New Smyrna with the mail, and, calling all the boys around him, read to them the following, from the columns of a well-known paper published in New York:—

Our Florida Expedition. — Just as we had begun to bewail the probable loss of our Commissioner at the bottom of the deep blue sea, we were gladdened by the announcement of his safe arrival at Mosquito Inlet, Indian River, and two days subsequently at New Smyrna, Florida, after a tedious passage of twenty-five days from Barnstable, Mass., in a coasting vessel.

St. Lucie will be the headquarters of our correspondent. Thence he will penetrate inland, and explore regions almost inaccessible, including Lake Okeechobee, of which latter he has already written extensively and minutely in these columns. These investigations will continue until April, and be aided by all necessary attendants and apparatus. He has two boats, tents, two men, the complete ordinary outfit of a sportsman, photographic apparatus, with one hundred negatives, and a stock of artist's materials, — all of which were taken with him from New England, — and also an Indian and native Florida guide, with swamp ponies, etc. His labors include commissions to collect specimens of Natural History and Indian relics for the Smithsonian and other scientific institutions. Altogether, the expedition is fitted out at considerable expense, and for the object sought to be accomplished, will prove itself eventually of considerable importance, and attach some credit to the enterprise of this Journal, under whose auspices alone it has been instituted. Both government and private enterprise have essayed explorations from time to time into the interior of Florida; but the information gained has been so far of little practical value or benefit, even when most needed, as it was during the seven years' Seminole War. How frequently we shall be able to hear from our correspondent, we cannot say, as there will be intervals of time when access to mail facilities will be impossible. However, the material furnished will be voluminous in the aggregate. He will write over the signature of "The Historian."

"Well, old fellow," he said, turning to the leader of the expedition, "what do you say to that? You didn't tell me you were out here under the auspices of a newspaper."

"No," returned the leader (who will be hereafter designated as the "Historian"), — "no, I did not, because I thought, as has now been shown, that the paper could 'speak for itself, John,' as an ancestor of yours once similarly remarked."

"That is true; but is it your expedition, or is it theirs? One would think by reading this item that theirs was the whole risk and expense of the entire exploration; but from what I have known of newspapers in general, they allow somebody else to do the work, and claim all the credit. Come, now, isn't it so in this case?"

"You are not far wrong, Major. To tell the plain truth, I have got seven hundred dollars invested in this enterprise, and the entire amount pledged by the great journal doesn't reach one hundred."

"Just as I thought. But why do you let them do it?"

"Oh, well, it doesn't hurt me, and the paper seems to enjoy it. Its subscription list will be increased, and its readers have a taste of new adventures."

"Perhaps you are right," returned the Major. "It is better to take these things philosophically; but I shouldn't like to do all the work and let another man get all the credit."

CHAPTER III.

AMONG THE LIVE-OAKERS.

THE good Major did not relax his energies, nevertheless, and saw them off in "first-rate style," as he put it; and they left him standing on his wharf, with a feeling akin to homesickness.

The next edition of the —— —— contained a description of the voyage down the lagoon, from the pen of the Historian. It opened as follows: —

We had what might be called a stormy voyage. The very night that saw the "Virginius" in such peril, we sighted the light off "Frying-pan Shoals," — just caught a glimpse of it, only to be driven away far east of the Gulf Stream. Four times did we cross the Gulf Stream. For a week we lay to under double reef-spanker and foresail, drifting with the waves. Dolphins and porpoises, gulf-weed and Portuguese men-o'-war, swam and drifted in the water near us; but they failed to excite the interest they ought, for the reason that the objects we sought on the shores of Florida were far away. The New Year brought a blessing; for upon that day we first descried the long low line, far in the distance, that told us of the land we sought. The next day the palms appeared above the horizon; but it was sunset ere we were boarded by the pilots and were threading the tortuous windings of the channel, in tow of the little steamer belonging to the port.

Mosquito Inlet, our destination, is in about latitude 29°, longitude 81°, fifty-five miles south of St. Augustine, and one third the way down the Florida coast. It is about a mile in width, with two channels, obstructed by sand-bars, having a depth of seven to nine feet. It is the outwatering of two large lagoons, — the Mosquito North, or Halifax River, and the Mosquito South, or Hillsborough River. Thirty miles each lagoon extends, meeting in a common channel at the inlet. Close in is Massacre Bluff, with its tragical history of the murder of shipwrecked sailors by Indians early in the Indian war. Two miles farther is Mount Pleasant, — a high shell-bluff, upon which is the residence of Major Alden, a Massachusetts man, whose hospitality many have shared. A mile farther is Lowd's Hotel, — the only one here, and one of the three houses constituting the town of New Smyrna. This place is about thirty miles from the St. John's, at Enterprise, the road to which fully maintains the reputation of Florida roads generally.

Though to a stranger the hotel at New Smyrna may present few attractions, being fronted by a muddy creek and backed by a dense forest, it is filled to overflowing every winter, the same boarders forming its quota each succeeding year, coming here to enjoy the superb fishing and get a shot at the game in the woods, — deer, bear, panther, and wild-cats.

The only business of New Smyrna is in live-oak, which, in the hands of one firm, employs many schooners the entire winter. On both lagoons are large groves of delicious oranges, noted for their size and flavor. The guava, pomegranate, fig, and banana will flourish here, and have been successfully grown.

The best location for building or camping is at Mount Pleasant, where the channel runs close by the wharf, with sixteen feet of water. We camped there upon its shelly shore, and passed two pleasant weeks, — pleasant, though I could not but heave a sigh whenever I thought of my field of labor so far away. The weather was unusually cold, even closing the jaws (if they have jaws) of the bloodthirsty mosquitoes for a time, and causing that omnipresent oldest inhabitant to declare with fearful imprecations that no such had occurred before since the great frost of '35. Yet we would have days delicious in their dreamy warmth, when the air of a morning would be full of the music of robin and red-bird.

"We" comprehends myself and a young man, — a friend, of my own age, who was to accompany me upon my boat excursions, and remain at camp while I was absent upon my explorations inland. "We," then, had a tent that had done service on the St. John's, which I had brought more for the good it had done than from any love I bore it. It was called the "lawn tent," and resembled the tents figured as belonging to the children of Israel. It was well adapted to the covering of a large surface; but in a "norther" we had to get out guys in every direction, and then stand outside and hang on, while the winds howled and the floods descended. We had two boats. I had one built to carry a heavy load in shallow water, and told her builder to sacrifice everything else to strength and lightness; and he did. She was twenty-one feet long by seven feet beam amidships, flat bottom, centre-board, rigged with two small sails. I had always stood in awe of her, and was much relieved when after she had lain idle nearly two weeks, a rash sailor asked me if he could sail her; and when he came back and said she worked splendidly, I could have embraced him. When the boat was loaded with our freight, I saw the wisdom of my instructions to the builder; for she was full to overflowing. And so, one pleasant day, we started down the Hillsborough, laden almost to the water's edge. We were fortunate in getting a tow down the river for nearly twenty miles.

The Hillsborough for twenty miles is filled with mangrove and marshy islands, making many exceedingly tortuous channels, difficult to follow. "Shipyard Reach," fifteen miles south of Smyrna, is a noted place for ducks.

The Mosquito Lagoon commences at the "Devil's Elbow," a channel of the Hillsborough where there are nine crooks in half a mile. We passed safely through the Devil's Elbow, and arrived at the headquarters of the Swifts, proprietors of the live-oak interest here. From Captain Swift and his employees we have received the kindest attention. Mosquito Lagoon is here two miles in breadth, and ten miles to the canal connecting this lagoon system with Indian River.

The live-oak is, or has been, one of the most valuable of our forest trees,— so valuable that the Government has protected and preserved large tracts or reservations of it in Florida, where no person is allowed to cut any timber. It is used altogether in ship-building; and the knees, or ribs, of vessels made from it will last a hundred years or more. There are yet shown on Cumberland Island, near the coast of Georgia, the stumps of trees from which were shaped the timbers of the frigate "Constitution," so celebrated in our history.

The live-oak is fast decreasing in numbers, and men are yet employed in cutting its valuable timber, which is shipped to the various navy-yards and stored up for future use.

At Captain Swift's camp three hundred men were employed, and they lived in little villages of palmetto huts, each group having its captain, teamster, and cook. They all were Northern men, most of them from the lumber camps of Maine,— men born in the woods, and well accustomed to fatigue. At first the oaks were cut upon the banks of the lagoon; but these were soon exhausted, and, mile after mile, the men had followed, building roads of logs across the marshes, and rude bridges over the creeks and swamps, until they had finally reached the margin of oak growth, seven miles away. There was no other village near; and this settlement, with its many huts, huge barns (for all hay and provender for the cattle had to be brought from the North), stores, warehouses, and wharfs, would be abandoned as soon as the supply of timber was exhausted.

Every morning a gang of men went into the woods; a certain number cut down the huge oak; others hewed the logs square, cut out the "knees," or bent limbs, which are the most valuable, and marked on every piece its contents in cubic feet. The timber was then taken by the teamsters, who hung them under the axles of their huge wheels, eight feet in diameter, and drew them to the river. Their teams contained six, eight, and sometimes ten yoke of cattle; and they were often nearly a day in accomplishing the distance to the lagoon. The native cattle were used, as, though hardly half the size of Northern oxen, they could undergo more fatigue, could travel more quickly and surely among the stumps and roots, and could live on less food. After the timber had been taken to the banks of the lagoon, it was loaded upon huge, boat-like rafts, and thence taken to the live-oak schooners, generally in waiting inside the bar at the inlet.

Captain Swift, a native of New Bedford, in Massachusetts, and his clerk, George Weld, took charge of us on our arrival, and introduced us to the interesting features of live-oaking. They were then cutting over an old indigo plantation, where the growth of live-oak is nearly or quite one hundred years old, on old fields that were once completely cleared. This old field was once cultivated by the famous Minorcan colony that was brought out here by Dr. Turnbull, over a century since. Ruins of the old buildings may be seen to-day back of New Smyrna. Turnbull Castle was on an elevation near the hotel, back of which are the old fields once planted with indigo; and remains of great canals, and wells, walled with coquina, or shell-rock, are found on every side.

The Antiquarian (the second member of the party) was deeply interested in everything pertaining to the history of Florida; and, to his great joy, he was introduced to one of the oldest residents of New Smyrna, Mrs. Sheldon, who lived here in 1835, when the place was attacked by the Seminoles. It was the day before Christmas that the Indians burst from the forest and set fire to all the buildings at three o'clock in the morning. Mrs. Sheldon escaped on a raft, under cover of the darkness, to a point south, just as the Indians reached the mouth of the creek. All the white people collected at "Bulow's," and there picketed themselves in, remaining close prisoners for six weeks, during which period occurred the fight at Dunbarton. The Indians began burning at New Smyrna, and followed the short line of settlements northward to St. Augustine; and when the United States troops arrived, there was no property for them to

AN EPISODE OF THE SEMINOLE WAR.

save. Mrs. Sheldon saw the famous Osceola many times; he was then about thirty years old, tall and fine-looking. The other Seminole chieftain — Coacoochee, or Wild Cat — was not so frank in his bearing as Osceola, but wild and sulky-looking. After most of the Seminoles had been captured, many of them poisoned themselves sooner than leave the country. Mothers poisoned their children with a certain tea they extracted from a root dug in the swamps.

The great Seminole war of fifty years ago, during which so many lives were lost and so much treasure wasted, was provoked by the aggressions of the white men, especially the cow-boys, who stole the land of the Indian and then his cattle.

Both Historian and Antiquarian were eager to learn more of live-oaking; and one morning, hearing that an ancient pike-head (a relic probably of the Spaniards of three hundred years ago) could be obtained at the cutters' camp, they started on foot through the woods, — first through the open pine-barren, with several wet "slews" in it bridged over, then through a swamp, over a bridge of cypress trunks seven eighths of a mile in length, then a mile farther through "hammock" and wet prairie. Everywhere were birds, — robins, blackbirds, red-birds, woodpeckers, and ground-doves. Violets, honeysuckles, oxalis, and blackberry bloomed on every side.

The choppers' shanties were more open than those of the teamsters, which were near the lagoon, and were in the midst of a beautiful hammock. Everything was well appointed, the food abundant and well cooked; and two cooks were in charge, while the choppers worked a mile away. There were three gangs of choppers, each containing forty-seven men; their first camp four miles from the lagoon, the second six, and the third eight miles away. To reach the timber, over five miles of corduroy bridges had been built; the longest bridge, seven eighths of a mile, was constructed in nine days, by a gang of two hundred men.

Two hundred yoke of oxen were employed in the woods, hauling out the timber, each yoke travelling some fourteen miles a day. The "drafts" used to haul out timber are great wheels nine feet in diameter, used in pairs, each pair drawn by five yoke of oxen. Fifty teamsters had charge of this force of cattle; and at the headquarters were extra drivers, clerks, carpenters, stablemen, and blacksmiths, all comfortably housed and busily employed.

Live-oaking was first carried on by the Swifts nearly seventy years ago, in Georgia, and has been kept up ever since by father and sons, operating chiefly upon the Sea Islands of Georgia. They have cut live-oak in Louisiana, Georgia, and central and eastern Florida. They came to Florida forty years ago, operating upon the North Lagoon, or Halifax River, until driven away by the Rebels, who destroyed their steamer and sixty thousand feet of live-oak. After the war was over they returned, and began work at this place. One should see all the different branches of the great work, each department in perfect order, to realize what has been accomplished by the indefatigable energy of these Northern men.

"NUMEROUS CHANNELS RUNNING OFF EAST AND WEST."

CHAPTER IV.

POTTERY AND PANTHERS.

THUS far the Historian has had it all his own way; now let the Antiquarian come to the fore. This chapter is his.

We tried to get under way from Major Alden's wharf about nine in the morning of January 16, having been shown the channel, with its devious wanderings, from the mast-head of the "Wandering Wind." But our attempt ended in total failure, owing to the small size of our rudder and to our having loaded the big boat too much "by the head." We only succeeded, after much trouble, in getting astern of a "lighter" (live-oak raft) and making fast to her. As the captain was going to the live-oak camp down the lagoon, and in our direction, we gladly accepted his invitation to "come aboard," and let events take their course.

When night came, he furnished us with sleeping-room on the floor under the bunks, where the water lapped and gurgled all night within a foot of our faces. But we slept very well, and next morning were off "Ship-yard Reach," where that immense shell-heap known as Turtle Mound looms up grandly above the ocean sand-ridge.

The lagoon, up to this point, is full of mangrove islands, with numerous channels running off east and west, so that it is very possible that any one unacquainted with the navigation here would get lost.

It had rained hard all night; but our boat was covered with a good canvas awning, so that the goods were not injured. Our large boat is loaded heavily, its rail within six inches of the water; but she floats easily, and will doubtless go through in good condition. She is pretty full, however; and boxes, trunks, barrels, rifles, guns, and oars are sticking up in strange confusion.

The sand-ridge intervening between the lagoon and the ocean is covered with a low growth of palmetto known as "scrub," with solitary palms here and there, and a few clumps of them at long intervals. It is all one general level, except for heaps of shells, like Turtle Mound, which are found, at long distances apart, rising above the sea of palmetto scrub. These mounds, sometimes of shell and sometimes of earth, are found scattered along both coasts of Florida.

The earth-mounds are said to have been erected ages ago as the sites for the royal residences of the caciques, or head chiefs. There is one between Indian River and Salt Lake; and an especially noteworthy one is that near Tampa, on the west coast of Florida, which was found by the soldiers of Pamphilo de Narvaez, and used as a royal residence of a great cacique when in 1528 Fernando de Soto arrived there on his expedition.

This Turtle Mound is covered with a dense growth of bayberry or similar shrub, intermixed with much Spanish bayonet, prickly-pear, and creeping vines of the convolvulus family. The summit is crowned with a few orange-trees and the same dense undergrowth. Its steepest incline is westward, and in some places is very steep, and presents the appearance of two hillocks separated by a narrow gully. It is composed of oyster, quahaug, and other shells, with a great deal of broken pottery intermixed.

While the slow lighter was lumbering along, I took the skiff and rowed to a high shell-bluff, where lived a Dr. Wallace, who hospitably entertained me and showed me the Indian mounds, old fields, and burial-grounds, back of the bluff, of which there are but a few acres in all.

The bluff is about forty feet high, in two hillocks, like Turtle Mound; and from the seaward side a depressed roadway led back to a level field, where I counted the sites of twenty shell-heaps.

The Doctor had a theory that this section, at the time of occupation by the Indians, was a mere sand-bar, and that the mounds were formed when there was little or no wood there. This he proved by showing layers of charcoal from burnt reeds and rushes found in excavations. These were the remains of fires upon which the Indians (as do the negroes of the present day) placed the oysters, to be opened by the heat. The oysters have not been found here for generations, the water of the lagoon is so salt; being so dense at times that even the fish are killed by thousands, particularly the cat-fish.

In these great shell-mounds many articles of metal, beads, and vast quantities of pottery have been found. The Doctor showed me a piece of gold, about an inch long, which he found in exhuming an Indian skeleton; and he gave me the skull which was dug up with it at the time.

On the next day the Historian and I found an old pike-head amongst the live-oakers, which was seven inches long and an inch and a half in breadth. It was covered with an eighth of an inch of rust, and was found about a foot beneath the surface of the ground. It was probably used by some member of one of the bands of Spaniards that ravaged this country three hundred years ago.

The Doctor had several tropical and semi-tropical trees growing near his house; but the most curious to me was the pawpaw, both wild and cultivated, which was bearing both fruit and flowers, and which he says is indigenous here, though this is the most northern point at which it is found wild.

There are but few houses along the banks of the lagoon. Perhaps the most interesting to me was the residence of Uncle Arad, whom we met first at New Smyrna. Uncle Arad was about seventy years old, about five feet high, and very much shrivelled. His pale blue eyes were sunken and watery; his beard gray with yellow tobacco stains. He had a peculiar habit of muttering to himself at odd times, when he would seem to be wholly abstracted, and would then gather up the hem of his coat, and holding it at half arm's-length would talk to it for hours at a time. At times he would look at me intently, all the while holding out his coat-skirt and talking at it. I once saw him on the beach thus occupied, and talking, apparently, to a duck. Every few steps as he walked along, he would stop and hold converse with his coat and whatever happened to be within range of his vision. Poor Uncle Arad! All his troubles began with a lightning-stroke in Texas, which killed his idolized wife, many, many years ago.

The Historian has described the live-oakers' camp, and it only remains for me to add such bits of information as he has left for my chapter.

By the time we had reached this point on our journey we were possessed of a veritable camping-out appetite; that is, we could sit down and eat all there was before us. And the coffee! As my cup holds nearly a quart, I had at first great difficulty in draining it at a sitting; but by this time that is a feat easily accomplished, and I regard it as a duty to see my face in its shining bottom at every meal. The provisions we brought from home were very welcome, especially the cookies and doughnuts, though the pies were soft and mouldy. I really don't know how we shall get along without mother's pies; six months without pie is a terrible prospect to contemplate!

It was interesting to learn from Captain Swift that he saw the great naturalist Audubon, when he was in Florida; but he remembered only that he was clad in a buckskin hunting-shirt, had a gun as long as himself, and was very dirty. He was alone, as usual. The Swifts were then beginning work upon the same great hammock they have just now finished. Forty years working in one tract of woodland! It was here, doubtless, that Audubon got his episode (related in his Biography) of the Adventures of a Live-oaker.

The Historian and I went out hunting frequently, but met with no great success. A Mr. Lewis, a famous hunter here, told us he saw a "tiger" in the road between New Smyrna and Enterprise, some time ago. It was about nine feet long, with a dark brown body, tail tipped and head barred with black. Upon seeing Mr. Lewis the panther stopped and looked at him, then cantered along leisurely ahead of him.

Panthers are killing all the deer about this section, and are very troublesome. The deer are still very numerous, and the best time to hunt them is in midwinter. The bucks drop their horns about February, March, and April, when the does have their fawns. By the end of August the fawns are weaned, and the does in fine condition; but the bucks are poor, and are at their best between October and February, especially about New Year's. One may often find their cast-off horns in the woods, and see trees with the bark scraped off by the bucks when rubbing their horns "in the velvet," when they are growing.

In the "piny woods" there are rattlesnakes, and in the swamps the moccasons, both very poisonous. One of the hunters we employed was poisoned by being scratched by the fang of a rattlesnake he had shot and was drawing out of the bushes after it was dead. Though he cut the end of his finger off, and tied up his arm to stop the circulation, he nearly died before reaching home, where he drank all the whiskey he could find, and barely saved his life.

The opinion in Florida is, that the poison fang is dangerous so long as it exists, and that the head ought to be burned at once after the reptile is killed.

The customary antidotes for rattlesnake venom are said to be, a solution of bread soda in water, to bathe the wound with and to drink, and equal parts of the white of an egg, salt, and powder, to be bound on the wound and renewed every few hours. A West-Indian remedy is to cut open a live chicken and bind it upon the wound while warm and bleeding. Whiskey, it seems, is the best thing to drink, except a solution of ammonia, and a great deal of the spirits is needed then to intoxicate. The limb, if an arm or leg is bitten, should be tied tightly above the bitten spot. The Seminole Indians have a remedy they call *pah-sah* (or rattlesnake-master),—a small plant, the root of which they chew to a pulp and bind at once upon the incision made by the fang.

It is the prevailing opinion that a rattlesnake will always give the alarm by rattling before he strikes. But this alarm cannot be depended upon, as the

THE NATURALIST IN FLORIDA.

snake will sometimes strike first and rattle afterwards. A dog belonging to one of the hunters saw one day a rattlesnake gliding along, and pounced upon it, when the snake turned and bit it, and then rattled half a minute later. The dog lived but two hours, although everything was done to save its life, such as cauterizing the wound and flashing powder into it.

The old naturalist Bartram, who came to Florida in the last century, would never kill a rattlesnake, calling it a generous animal that never struck at man without giving the alarm. But it must have deteriorated in the past hundred years; and it will always be best to kill the snake at sight.

Of all the animals of these woods that have the power to harm man and do not freely use it, perhaps the panther is the most generous. Captain Swift says that he and his brother once passed a panther in the woods, as they were riding, that only sat up and snarled at them. After they had gone some way, they tied their horses and were looking at some timber, when they saw the animal coming towards them, evidently following in their tracks. The Captain picked up a handspike, and shied it at the beast (it came so near), when it drew itself up and snarled horribly, but soon bounded into the bushes and disappeared. Two of the axemen, at work in a hammock, were "squaring" a great live-oak log they had felled, and very intent upon their work, when a panther crept stealthily up, drew their dinner off the end of the log, bolted it, and disappeared. They were so frightened that they ran all the way to camp.

This event occurred a few days before our arrival; but the panther episode most talked about was one in which figured Jim Seobie, an old Indian River guide. We asked Jim for the particulars, and he told us all about it: —

"It was on Pelican Island. I was down thar durin' the last trouble with the Injuns, an' was a-huntin' pink curlew, that used to breed thar, for the officers of the rigiment at Fort Capron. I was a-goin' along, a-shootin' on the wing, an' lookin' up more 'n down, when all of a suddin I see two fiery eyes a-looking at me outen a clump of mangroves. Then I saw somethin' movin', and see another pair, an' knew to oncet they was both panthers. Wall, I slipped back, an' rammed in two buck-shot wire cartridges, and one of these I fired at the fust panther, an' killed him dead. The other, he run off, an' I let him have hit, an' he drapped. That's all there is to my panther story. Yaas, there's plenty in these hammocks, an' you youngsters may run across 'em yit, before you git back this yer way ag'in."

CHAPTER V.

A HUNT FOR TURTLE-EGGS.

OLD Jim Scobie, the panther hunter, took a hold upon our affections at once by his blunt, honest ways, and won our admiration by his great skill in sailing our boat and in hunting. So we made a bargain with him to go with us to the end of Indian River Lagoon, sail our boat, provide the camp with game, and act as our guide.

Jim only asked for time to run over to his little hut and place a stick against the door, after he had got his rifle and haversack; and it was early in the morning that we set sail from the live-oak camps, and made directly for the "haul-over." This "haul-over" is the point where the two great water-systems of the East Florida coast, the Mosquito Lagoon and the Indian River, approach nearest. There used to be a path here, over which the early navigators hauled their boats from one lagoon to the other; but now there is a canal, dug by Government, and boats of light draught can go through with little detention.

There are several orange groves on this lagoon, both wild and cultivated. We entered the canal about noon one day, passing the first stake half a mile north, and standing away southeast till opposite the canal. The eastern end is invisible till directly at its mouth, owing to bushes and sand-bars. The canal is about half a mile long and twelve feet wide. Connecting the Indian River Lagoon with the Mosquito, it forms with them an inside route of water travel over one hundred and eighty miles in length. The water was at the highest when we entered, yet we barely passed through, drawing but a foot. Fallen coquina has narrowed the passage to seven feet in some places. The coquina is curiously hollowed by the water, leaving overhanging arches supported by

"A PANTHER CREPT STEALTHILY UP"

fantastically wrought pillars. The kingfisher has driven his shafts into the rock, and then occupied them. A large tree, with table-shaped top, stands near the eastern end, and can be seen a long way, forming a conspicuous landmark. There is good camping-ground near here, and an abundance of fish and ducks close by. Deer and bear range the hammocks north.

We camped that night at Andrew Jackson's. Andrew had the neatest little orange grove on the river. Close by, two miles, is the famous Dummitt orange grove, so often described. Captain Dummitt, the original owner of this grove, is now dead. He was an old resident, and highly respected. The grove is now owned by his three daughters and two others. It is about sixteen miles from the canal to the head of the river, and ten miles to Sand Point, upon the west bank of the river.

In these lagoons and at the inlets, where openings are found to the ocean, the water really swarms with fish. The mullet were most abundant, swimming in shoals, and taken only by the cast-net, as they will not bite the hook.

Many of the fish found in Florida have Spanish names, such as the crevalli, which sometimes weigh seven pounds apiece, and the pompano, taken by the net. Then there are the blue-fish, which afford excellent sport, the sargent-fish, jew-fish, bass, or red-fish, salt-water trout, red-snapper, sheep's-head, king-fish, toad-fish, croaker, and blow-fish.

The shark, especially in the deep channels and in the breakers on the beach, were very ravenous, and would frequently bite a large bass in two, after it was caught, and while it was being hauled in.

A walk on the ocean beach revealed many new and curious denizens of the sea, washed upon the shore, or recently caught. None attracted their attention more curious than the quaint porcupine fish (*Diodon hystrix*), which, when freshly found, looked like an inflated pin-cushion.

Sea-shells of many varieties are cast up here by the waves, and several vegetable products of the West Indies, as cocoanuts and sea-beans. These latter grow in the forests in the West India islands, fall into the streams, and are carried by the currents to the shores of Florida. There they are found in great numbers, collected, polished, and sold by curiosity-venders to tourists as watch-charms and ornaments. Probably no more fragile form of sea-life came before their notice than that known as the sea-butterfly. A ramble anywhere along the beach on the ocean side of the ridge gave numerous specimens to be added to the collections of the Historian and the Antiquarian.

In the groves and gardens there were not only oranges, but lemons, limes, citrons, pawpaws, guavas, shaddocks, pine-apples, peaches, pomegranates, alligator pears, and bananas.

The scrub and thickets were alive with small birds, and the air with larger ones, — gulls, terns, and pelicans; while the eagles and fish-hawks were just beginning to construct their bulky nests of sticks.

On the beach the turtles would soon begin to lay their eggs. The season for turtles' eggs begins, generally, in May or June; but Jim, our guide, was confident that we could find some this early if we should care to make a search on the ocean beach. Jim had come in from an interview with one of the settlers, and had been informed that turtles had been seen on the beach.

It is a wonderful region, — that long stretch of sand that separates the lagoons of the east coast of Florida from the ocean. It is nearly three hundred miles in length, broken here and there by a river that forces itself through, — in some places five miles in breadth, in others but a few hundred yards across. It is mainly covered with scrub and low trees, interspersed with saw-palmetto and thorny plants, and is the home of many deer, wild-cats, panthers at times, and hordes of raccoons and 'possums. Rattlesnakes are often met with here, and make things lively for an inexperienced hunter who hears their rattle for the first time.

This was good news that Jim brought us, — that bears were walking the beach, — for bears never walk the ocean beach without an object, and that object is *turtle-eggs*. The bears live in the great cypress swamps of the west side of the river, crossing to the coast at the season of turtle-laying, never a week too soon or too late. They are good swimmers, but are sometimes overtaken and killed in the water. Only the week before, one had been pursued by some men in a boat. The men caught up with him, and one of them made a blow at him with a hatchet, when he turned about and attacked the boat, getting one paw over the rail. The men were frightened and desisted, wisely concluding it better to let him escape than to run the risk of swamping the boat.

To return to the camp: "Bears is walkin'," said Jim, "and turtles is crawlin'; and if we don't give both a lively time, jest put me down for an apple-blossom." When Jim was particularly sanguine about anything, he always made the modest request to be recorded as an apple-blossom in case of failure.

We ate breakfast, and then took our guns and went to the beach, where the great waves came in tumultuously and dashed up the smooth sand. He walked ahead, and I followed in his tracks until we reached a spot where the sand was softer, and we sank ankle-deep. "There! don't you see them tracks, jest like you'd stuck the top of your head in the sand? Them's bear-tracks. Now look here," continued he, going farther down, and calling my attention to

FISHING FOR THE HAMMER-FISH.

a broad trail that led up from the water to near the border of beach-grass, "that's a turtle-track."

Two deep grooves were drawn in the sand by the turtle's fins as it had drawn its heavy body up the sand, between which was a broad furrow made by the body itself. The turtle had floundered over the sand with apparently aimless intent, and had gone back to the sea without depositing her eggs, seemingly not satisfied with the spot.

The bear had come up from the south along the beach, and had stopped here and dug in several places, misled by the turtle's trail into the belief that she had laid her eggs here; from this point he had gone off into the scrub to look for oysters on the river-shore, Jim said. "No matter; they'll both be back to-night somewhere within a half a mile of this very place: the turtle'll be back to lay her eggs, the bear'll be back to look after the turtle, and we — we'll be here to look after the bear." Saying which, with a chuckle, Jim led the way up the beach to look for fresh tracks.

We found another trail, but no eggs, though all our observations showed us that there was a good prospect for the night. There was a moon that night, — a moon that flooded even the dark grove where our hammocks were hung; and as we reached the beach equipped for spending at least half a night on the sand, it was almost as light as day. It was about eight o'clock when we reached the spot we had first examined. I was posted there, and Jim hastened on a mile farther.

A tangled mass of scrub palmetto, with thick roots and broad leaves, overhung an excavation in a sand-bank; near and beneath this, in a hollow and in deep shade, I took my seat. No sound broke upon the air except that of the surf; not a living or moving object was in sight in all the long stretch of beach I could command on either side of me.

Spreading an old coat upon the sand, I sat down with my gun across my knee and waited. Our desire was to get the turtle as she left for the sea after leaving her eggs, and also to identify the exact spot in which she placed them. After the eggs are once buried in the sand, this is no easy matter, as there is nothing to indicate their presence. Experienced egg-collectors walk the beach, in the season, with long rods in their hands, with which they probe the sand; they can tell by the looseness or firmness of the sand whether it has been recently disturbed, and at once dig when they find a difference in the resistance offered.

One hour, two hours, I waited. It was getting cold, and I was growing tired. Up and down the beach I looked, and saw nothing but the white surf and sand. Nothing? A dark object at that moment seemed to rest in the surf

Watching it, I defined it growing into shape, and emerge upon the sand. Very slowly it moved up the sand; inch by inch its huge bulk was carried on, till it was half-way up the beach. It was three hundred yards away; but I did not seek to lessen the distance between us, for fear it would return to the sea at sight of me. When it had reached its destination and begun to dig, would be the safest period.

"SEIZING A FLIPPER AND LAYING HOLD BENEATH THE UPPER SHELL."

At last it seemed to have settled upon a spot to its mind, and commenced to fling the sand about with its hind flippers. Soon it had nearly hidden itself, and had dug a burrow, by the time I reached it, nearly three feet deep. At my approach it protruded its head and gave utterance to a hissing noise, but did not offer to escape, and I stood watching it while it laid its eggs in the hole. This took a long while, for there must have been nearly a hundred, and I was beginning to get impatient, when it seemed to conclude it had done its

duty for that night, and crawled out of the hole. It then carefully covered the eggs with sand, smoothing the place of deposit over with as much care as though one of her enemies had not been watching her all the time, and then prepared to depart.

"Now, madam," thought I, "is my turn, — my turn to turn you over!" The sea-turtles, once turned upon their backs, cannot regain their feet; consequently it is only necessary to turn one over to capture it for good and all. Seizing a flipper, and laying hold beneath the upper shell, I bore my strength against it; but in vain, — I could not make it budge an inch. The turtle was not inactive all this time; for it was scratching desperately, throwing up great showers of sand, which nearly blinded me, and all the while working its way towards the sea.

I shouted for Jim; but he was far out of hearing, and I was obliged to struggle on alone. It was humiliating to have to give up. I could at least, I thought, prevent the turtle from reaching the water till Jim's arrival. But though I exerted all my strength, she gradually lessened the distance between herself and the water, and finally was within a rod of it.

A thought struck me: if I could shoot her in the head, I might wound her badly enough to stop her, if it did not kill. I started up the beach for my gun, where I had left it leaning against the bank, seized it, and darted back — just as the water closed over the turtle's back.

This was an awful disappointment; our turtle-steaks had gone to sea, but the eggs were left. Digging them out, however, was not so easily nor so quickly done as I had imagined it would be. With my hands I could not begin to make the progress the turtle had made with her flippers; but after a while they lay uncovered, and I drew out, one after another, eight dozen eggs. These eggs were about two inches in diameter, white, covered with a leathery skin; they are not so good, in my opinion, as the eggs of a fowl, having a *mealy* feeling in the mouth.

I laid the eggs in a pile, and waited for Jim. It was an hour before he came along, swinging in his hand an opossum he had captured in the scrub. His disappointment was great; but when I showed him the track of the turtle, and the evidences of our struggle, he agreed that the turtle must have been an immense one, and that he could have done no better himself, alone and unassisted. He then took off his jacket, tied up the sleeves, and filled it with the turtle-eggs, and we carried them to camp between us.

He remarked to me, as we marched along: "The bear ain't been here to-night, that's cert'in; but he's goin' to be here to-morrer. I'm willin' to bet a heap on it."

Jim was always willing to "bet a heap on to-morrer." He looked forward cheerfully to " to-morrer " as a time of possible pleasure.

We did not give Jim that coveted " to-morrer," not being so sanguine as he was; but a fair wind springing up, we set sail the next night for Sand Point, on the western bank of the Indian River.

CHAPTER VI.

DOWN THE INDIAN RIVER.

WE crossed the river one night, after waiting two days for a wind. The water was all aglow with phosphorescent light. Every dash of our little boat raised a silver shower, and thousands of fish darted hither and thither, leaving tortuous trails of fire, like those Fourth of July serpents of our boyhood. Rafts of ducks sprang up with noise like thunder; invisible, but for the fiery shower they raised upon leaving the water.

It was the Antiquarian who went for turtle-eggs over to the ocean beach. The Historian, during his absence, explored one of the creeks near the camp in his skiff. During this trip he declared he was a witness to one of those episodes in animal life that seem to warrant the belief that many birds are possessed of higher attributes than are generally accorded to them, and have something more than mere instinct.

His attention was called to a disturbance among the mangroves of a little islet near, and soon there flapped into view a black duck, a female, evidently wounded. Close in her wake followed a sly-looking coon, his attention so occupied with the duck as not to notice the Historian till fairly in view. Then he hesitated; but the duck brushed so near his nose that he again took up the pursuit, throwing a glance occasionally at the Historian. It was interesting to watch them; keeping just ahead of her pursuer, the duck would beat the water quickly all the time in evident pain, and would so delude the old fellow that he finally seemed to think of nothing else but catching her. What a puzzled expression his shrewd face wore, when, after nearly placing his paw upon her, she would escape! Then he would stop, look at the Historian as if to say, "What the deuce does all this mean?" and arching his back, would again pursue with long leaps. For over a quarter of an hour did the duck play with him, till having enticed him a sufficient distance from her nest, she flew away. If ever the face of a sharp-nosed coon wore a sheepish look, it was the face of that same coon. And the Historian afterward acknowledged: "I accelerated his sneaking trot by a charge of duck-shot."

The moon went down as we reached Sand Point. We arose next morning, and looked about us. There had been little change since the Historian was first here, about two years before; but different people occupied the shops and boats, and there were few familiar faces.

Jim, our guide, here met an old acquaintance, and improved the day of leisure here by going off on "a time," returning at night in a state of garrulous inebriety. He insisted upon telling us how it was he had the fight with the Seminoles, and why Charley Osceola had his hand slit. This is the way he began: —

"Well, now, lemme tell you. You see, Charley and me, we got drunk, and he told me something on Tommy Tiger, and then I told it, and that made trouble.

"What was it I told? Well, lemme tell you. Charley, he said Tommy kill white man, long time ago. So, when Tommy come in — he'd been hunting out to Okeechobee — I said to him, 'You miserable red rascal! you kill white man.' And he said, 'How you know?' And I said, 'Charley told me:' and then he and Tommy Tiger was mad right off.

"What happened then? Well, lemme tell you. Charley, he come to me and wanted to kill me, and I said, 'You red fool, you, I kill you!' and we got to fighting, and Sim Smith, — he was drunk too, — he undertook to stop us, and grabbed Charley by the throat, who bit a chunk right out of Sim's hand.

"Then the squaws come up and tied Charley and me, and then we cooled off. But, lemme tell you, next time Charley got drunk, he just went for me and wanted to fight; but I got him quiet by telling him I had a bottle of whiskey out in the scrub, and he went out with me, and when he had his drink, I just hit him on the head with a billet of wood, and told him just to keep still after this, and let me alone.

"Well, lemme tell you. 'T wa'n't long after this before we both got drunk ag'in, and he got after me and I tried to cut his lights out of him. Then the squaws tied us both up to trees, and the mosquitoes nearly eat us up before the old hags cut us loose ag'in.

"Did the tribe take any notice of it? Well, lemme tell you. They just held a council of war, when they all got back to Miami; and old Tiger Tail, he split Charley's hand open.

TIGER TAIL.

"Did n't he object? Well, lemme tell you. What could he do? It was either to have his ears cut off smooth, or his nose cut off, or his hand slit. He thought he'd rather have his hand slit, and so 't was done. Then he had to go off by himself for one full moon. Tommy Tiger, he was afraid I'd tell of what he'd done, and write to the Great Father at Washington, and so he never bothered me any more."

This authentic narration of Jim's exploits will give the reader some sort of conception of the guide we had. His wild freaks had given him a reputation throughout the whole coast region; he was feared and admired by all the rough residents of this section, who generally allowed him to do as he pleased. We could get no other man who would undertake to pilot us through to Lake

Okechobee, however, and so we put up with his vagaries; only giving him as few chances as possible to get at the whiskey-bottle.

The region about Sand Point presented a succession of beaches and bays, with whitest sand, and coquina rock overtopped by palmettos. The settlement was not a large one, comprising a hotel, boarding-house, and a few score houses; but it was then the most important on the river. Since our visit Sand Point has been connected with the St. John's by a railroad, and a steamer runs up and down the river, or lagoon; but at that time the nearest point of the St. John's region was Salt Lake, six miles away, and the only water-craft were sloops and schooners.

The white lines of sand between the blue water and the green hammocks give a beautiful effect to the shores all along the lagoon.

The "hammocks" consist mainly of oaks and pines, and they are the darkest green of all the clumps of trees along the shore.

This term "hammock" may need to be explained to some readers; hence what follows below:—

"An old writer classifies the land of Florida under the heads, 'pine, *hammock*, savanna, swamp, marsh and bay, or cypress galls.' He mentions the existence in the hammocks of '*chamærops frondibus palmatis plicatis, stipitibus ferratis*, of whose fruit all animals are very fond.' He says the pine-barrens receive their name from the '*pinus foliis longissimus ex una theca ternis*.' I suppose any one with a clear head can see the difference between lands bearing such widely dissimilar trees, when the author so clearly states their specific names. Further, under the head of 'high' and 'low' hammock is comprised the richest land of Florida. For land that produces crops of cane year after year, the Floridian will choose hammock land. If I were writing a letter upon the agriculture of Florida, I might go on and describe the many advantages possessed by hammock land over the rest; but I am not, and find that instead of merely supporting myself in the use of the term 'hammock,' I have branched off into the relative merits of the peculiar qualities of Florida vegetation, soil, or what not, termed hammock and pine-land. Whether the term is confined to Florida or not, I am unable to say; but certain it is that it has a peculiar signification not possessed elsewhere. It may be applied to any clump of trees strikingly different from those surrounding it, as 'cabbage (palmetto) hammock,' 'live-oak hammock,' etc. Regarding soil, it is called 'shell,' if high and growing upon one of the many shell-heaps of Florida, or 'swamp,' if low and wet."

A LITTLE BAY BACK OF OLEANDER POINT.

The Historian interjects this item of information, as he is better acquainted with Florida's resources than the Antiquarian, who is supposed to be the writer of this chapter. But we will feel just as much obliged to him for the information as though he had been asked to contribute it. Some people are so full of knowledge, that they froth it over upon the slightest provocation.

The wind blowing through the palmetto tops makes a peculiarly angry sound, and is especially effective when lashing the broad leaves against their trunks. This was the sound we heard on the second morning at Sand Point; but our boatman decided to start, and we had to follow his advice. Before noon the wind was blowing heavily and the seas running high, and our small boat astern twice parted the line by which it was towed.

About mid-afternoon we were obliged to seek the shelter of a little bay back of Oleander Point. Here the coquina rock forming the shore is worn into a thousand fantastic shapes; the most curious, perhaps, was where the palmettos had grown out of it, leaving a hole the exact shape of the bole after it had been blown over; and not only this, but the various holes through which the roots and rootlets had penetrated, with their thousand ramifications. The beach is composed of disintegrated shells, white as snow, and forming a crescent-shaped bar running out into the water nearly half a mile. Hovering about this bar continually during the day, are those most graceful of sea-swallows, the roseate terns. Below our landing-place was an upturned boat, which had been wrecked in the gale, and its occupants drowned. It is said that Indian River can get up a heavier blow at shorter notice, than any other body of water of its size in the world.

The Historian stretched a rope between two palms, and threw a piece of canvas over it, fastening one side down against the sand and leaving an open front, where a fire was built, and we had a most comfortable shelter for the night.

The wind changed to the westward during the night, and we started at daylight down the river, reaching Elbow Creek in a couple of hours, into which we turned for shelter. As we went over the bar, a great wave struck us fairly in the back, setting some of our things afloat.

Mr. Houston, the resident at Elbow Creek, is an old Indian fighter, having served through the seven years of the first war. His reminiscences were interesting, especially to me, as he had fought Indians I had met at the Seminole town and while hunting, and had fought at localities I had recently visited.

A wedge-shaped coquina rock terminates Merritt's Island, two miles east of Elbow Creek. The rocky shores here are worn into innumerable caverns, their roofs supported by water-wrought pillars and groined arches. The island comes down to this point, ever narrowing, till it terminates a mile north of a palm-crowned point upon the eastern shore. A deep bay is formed, crescent-shaped, covered with dainty shells. Bordering this bay is a high shell-bluff, covered with wild orange-trees. Back of this bluff is an ancient earth-mound, from which leads an elevated roadway, sixty feet in width, to the sea beach a mile away.

On the extreme southern end of Merritt's Island, where the rocks are hollowed out in great caverns, and worn into every conceivable shape by the waves, a man named Stone had built himself a hut. "Old Stone"—as Jim called him—was not at home; so we inspected his shanty at our leisure. It was made of palmetto leaves, open at both ends, and filled with all sorts of old wrecking-stuff. The bed was merely a pen of boards, with old gunny-bags as bedding; while all the cooking utensils were outside, the kitchen being in the open air. The only domestic animals about were a cat and a herd of goats, the latter led by a ferocious old "Billy" with glaring eyes and branching horns.

The Historian thought this a good opportunity to try his camera and chemicals; and so, after a great deal of labor, the herd of goats was brought together near the hut, and the artist proceeded to focus the group. Just as he got his head under the focussing-cloth, old Billy started in his direction with such a determined air, and so suddenly, that the would-be photographer thought he wouldn't stay to complete that picture; to tell the truth, he hasn't finished it yet. About five minutes later, all of us were sitting on the fence, picking out of our legs the prickly-pear spines that had got stuck into them during our rapid retreat from the Billy-goat. As for old Billy, he overturned the photographer in one desperate charge, and then pranced up and down the enclosure, chasing first one of us, then the other, till we were all adorning the top rail of the fence and looking exceedingly foolish.

"Old Stone" evidently delighted in his island home; for he had built a nice landing-place, and laid out a walk along the eastern side, besides clearing a large space which he had left for the growth of tender sprouts for his goats. He had long rows of prickly-pear and other cacti, seemingly taking a great interest in their cultivation. He had lived here for years, and might well be termed the "Crusoe of Merritt's Island." He had no love for "Old Titus," the King of Sand Point, who, he said, should be buried with his face downward, so that the more he scratched the deeper he would go.

THE GREAT COLONY OF PELICANS.

Leaving this beautiful spot, where the beaches and bays were most attractive of any on the lagoon, we sailed on till near the Narrows, before entering which we made a side-trip to a mangrove island famous for its great colony of pelicans.

The pelican found on the east coast of Florida is the gray one, the *Pelicanus fuscus* of the ornithologists, while the great white pelican is rarely seen except along the west coast.

While coasting the numerous mangrove islets, we killed five blue-wing teal, and saw many hundreds of ducks and herons on the broad mud-flats. Flapping slowly above the surface of the water were the great gray pelicans, as big as geese, with their long bills and enormous pouches beneath. They grew more and more abundant, until at last the air was full of them, sailing around the low mangrove island which they had chosen as their home. This was their breeding-place; and not only were there hundreds of mature birds, but a great many young. The ground was covered with them, as well as the mangrove trees, which latter had long ago been killed by the great weight of the nests and the constant visits of the birds. The nests were bulky affairs, built of sticks, as big as a bushel-basket. Some nests contained eggs like goose-eggs in shape and size, and appearing as though they had been whitewashed. Of these eggs we collected nearly a hundred, in order to have a supply not only for our own collection, but for exchange with other naturalists at home.

It took us several hours to "blow" these eggs and clean them; and when the job was done it was nearly dark, and Jim declared — in his most emphatic way — that we must leave immediately, and set sail for the Narrows.

The wind again hauled northwest, and a heavy thunder-storm burst upon us at the entrance of the Narrows. It was dangerous navigation here, even in good weather and by daylight; but with a storm after us, and black clouds obscuring the moon, we felt that we were driving on to certain shipwreck. The channel was very narrow, and obstructed by long oyster-reefs, over which the boat's keel would frequently grate ominously. But there was no shelter on the east side of the lagoon; so we had to "trust to luck, and let her drive," with the storm thundering after us and a pelting rain drenching us to the skin.

Well along into the night, as we were sitting crouched under our tarpaulins, while Jim was at the tiller, we heard a sudden exclamation from that worthy, and looked out. "A bear!" he shouted, pointing to a black object in the water off the port bow. It was about thirty or forty yards away, and swimming directly down upon us. "And he's coming this way, boys! Get out your guns!"

The guns and revolvers had been packed in the trunks, out of the way of the rain, and we had nothing at hand but an axe. "Give it to me, then, quick! or he'll get his paws on the rail and tip the boat over! Take the tiller, one of you!"

One of us took it, while the other hunted for some weapon of defence, and Jim scrambled forward over the baggage to the bows. The wind was still blowing fiercely, and the rain falling in sheets, so that the boat was nearly unmanageable. It was only now and then that we could see the black object in the water, so gloomy and dark were the surroundings. At last we heard an excited cry from Jim, and then a dull thud. A black paw reached up and grasped the rail; but Jim's axe descended swiftly and it fell off, only to be followed by another, which another blow caused to relax its hold. For a while the bear struggled to get a hold on the boat, but repeated and well-directed blows on his head soon made him give it up.

He then floundered about awhile, the boat forged ahead, and we were obliged to leave him, desperately wounded, no doubt, but still with life enough to prove a dangerous customer at close quarters.

Jim then crawled back and took the helm, muttering curses upon "them Yankees" who didn't know enough to keep their fire-arms ready. "We might 'a' got that bear just as well as not, if you'd only had your rifle handy; and now," he snorted contemptuously, "there's twenty dollars gone to grass, to say nothing of the meat we might have had."

This episode kept us awake till a "lee" was made, and a shelter, when the boat was anchored and we crawled on shore to try to get a little sleep. With some splinters of light-wood Jim started a fire (after infinite trouble); and as the rain now fell less violently, we tried to dry our clothes. Failing in this, we warmed our chilled limbs, and then "turned in" in our saturated blankets, where we lay all night, with the rain pouring upon us.

At dawn, next morning, the wind was still blowing, though less heavily, the rain had ceased, and the waves were lower. We were cold and wet and stiff, and most grateful was the fire Jim revived from the embers. Over this we cooked flapjacks and potatoes, and made coffee, and then set sail for the east bank of the lagoon.

Following a devious channel amongst numerous mangrove islands, we at last met a strong current setting against us, and rounding a point found shelter near the mouth of Indian River Inlet. Across a spit of sand, a hundred yards, was the ocean surf, where the waves were breaking high, with thunderous sound. Landing on the sand, we spread our wet blankets and clothing out in the sun to dry, and basked happily in its warmth.

CHAPTER VII.

A BEAR-HUNT ON THE BEACH.

THIS chapter has been assigned to the Historian, who is an enthusiastic hunter as well as fisherman. He says: —

The termini of the beaches on either side of the inlet were two long points of sand, with the channel between, and a sand-bar over which the waves break high. On the north of the entrance lies the wreck of a steamer; on the south, the beach stretches away till lost in the distance, and above it hover thousands of terns, gulls, and pelicans.

On the southern spit, during the War of the Rebellion, a large number of Southern refugees encamped, among whom was our guide, Jim Scobie.

The inlet has three channels after breaking through the beach: one to the north and west, one to the southwest, the third due west, — a beautiful water-way, winding between banks of mangrove-trees.

The beaches were covered with shells, thickly strewn with Portuguese men-o'-war, and delicately cut sea-weeds.

We camped here two days, finding the best fishing we had ever met with. The first day was passed in fishing, drying our stores, and shooting the rarest of the sea-birds that hovered in clouds above the bar, and swam in the surf.

The memory of that day's sport will not soon fade away. Bass, sheep's-head, crevalli, — all bit well, and fully sustained the reputation accorded this inlet as the best fishing-ground on the coast. Jim had been hunting in the scrub along the sand-ridge, and returned to the boat as I hauled in my last fish. There was blood on his face, — blood on his hands, hair, and rifle. His shirt and pants were torn and likewise bloody. In reply to my questions he remarked in a careless way that he had run afoul of a catamount, and that "the beast had showed fight." When I requested him to bring along his catamount, he said that it was out there in the sand, and that if I wanted it I might get it. Though I had doubts of the existence of said catamount, I went as directed, and did actually find one, — a beautiful creature, about four feet in length, curiously spotted and striped, and with tufted ears. Jim had discovered four of them, and had wounded one and then captured him.

I again got out my photographic apparatus, and won the undying love of our guide by photographing him in the act of harpooning a shark.

It was just here that I encamped one night two years ago. Jim was with me, and performed a feat that many men would shrink from. The captain of a little schooner had got his anchor caught beneath a sunken mangrove, and was going to cut his cable and leave it, when Jim volunteered to dive for and get it up. The water was alive with sharks, — this place is noted for them, — and the anchor was twenty feet under water; but Jim, after giving me instructions in case he was attacked, dove repeatedly, with the sharks swarming about our little boat, and a rapid current running, till he had accomplished his purpose. So it was peculiarly fitting that I should photograph him in this heroic attitude of harpooning the dreaded monster of the deep.

But to return to the catamounts. There were plenty of them in the scrub, Jim averred, and all we need do to get a full line of specimens was to go into the scrub and hunt for them. This we did, but were not fortunate enough to find any; and the Antiquarian, when he returned to the boat, laid aside his gun and vowed he would devote himself solely to historical research and antiquities. But I was not satisfied. Having been here before, I knew that the beach scrub contained game enough to supply us not only with specimens but with meat for our larder. As a result of this conviction that there was sport ahead if we would only hunt for it, we encountered the following adventure.

Leaving the camp in charge of the Antiquarian, at sunset of the second day, Jim and I walked far up the beach, with our rifles. Why we went there, and what we got there, will appear below.

Beneath my feet, as I write, is a bear-skin, with long hair, shaggy and black; though from its appearance a hunter could tell that it was not a bear of the North, — its coat of fur is too thin, and it has not the gloss of the winter coat of a Northern bear. But it is the skin of a bear, for all that; and the sight of it carries me back to the second night of that camp on the Florida beach.

I had posted myself on the beach half a mile from camp, and Jim had chosen a position at an equal distance on the other side. Bears had begun to visit the beach in numbers, in search of turtle-eggs; during the day we had traced the

"BIRDS THAT HOVERED IN CLOUDS ABOVE THE BAR."

footsteps of three, and there was promise of great sport during the night. There was nothing simpler than the mode of hunting them: in their wanderings in search of eggs the bears followed the beach, examining a track of turtle here, stopping to dig there, — if successful, not travelling far; but if not, sometimes covering many miles. To get a shot at a bear, it was only necessary to choose a suitable ambush, possess yourself with patience, keep quiet, and pot the animal as he came along. It seemed simple and easy enough — But I anticipate.

An hour after sunset I was at my station, my rifle (which I had carefully cleaned and oiled in the afternoon) held in my hand, a dozen spare cartridges

TURTLE ON THE BEACH.

in a convenient pocket. I did not doubt my ability to kill a bear. So many times had I listened to the tales of hunters who had killed them, — who represented it the easiest thing possible, — that I had already slain many, in imagination.

I sat down there in perfect calmness, arranged the thick scrub that screened me from the observation of anything on the beach, and waited and listened. The moon, which left the water at sunset, mounted higher and higher, until it nearly reached the zenith, and I knew it was near midnight; and still no bear.

The measured beat of the ocean, as its waters fell heavily on the shore, lulled me to sleep at last, with its monotonous poundings. It was a glorious June night, warm and dewless; the perfume of palmetto blossoms and wild verbena hung heavy on the air.

Wrapped in my blanket, my rifle in the hollow of my arm, I leaned against a clump of bushes and fell asleep. With the consciousness, however, that it was my duty to keep awake, it was impossible to sleep soundly. Now and then I would awake and peer above the bushes, then relapse into slumber. The third or fourth time that I did this, as I was about settling myself back in my nest, I fancied I caught a glimpse of some object up the beach. Thinking that it was some creation of my sleepy brain, I yet ventured to assure myself by another glance, and was startled indeed to perceive a great black form slowly moving towards me. In an instant every sense was alert, and my heart was pounding away with an energy that nearly suffocated me.

That bear — for it was a bear — when he first hove in sight was a long distance off; but he soon decreased it, though he seemed to walk slowly. And how he loomed up! I had never imagined a bear could attain such a size. In my excited imagination he grew a foot in height for every rod he advanced; now he was as large as a donkey, now as large as a cow, and now he reached the dimensions of a small house. He grew so large as to obstruct the sea altogether, and I could see nothing but a strip of white sand, with that huge object moving swiftly down it to devour me.

Then I saw what a fool I had been to place myself in such a situation! Thoughts of safety had taken the place of those of glory to be obtained in the slaying of a bear, and I heartily wished myself back in camp. But this was impossible; a movement in any direction would betray me, and I could do nothing less than sit still, and, if too cowardly to fire, let the bear pass. Jim would then have a shot at him. This thought stirred me and touched me in a tender spot, — my pride. If I suffered that bear to pass without an attempt to stop him, I should never hear the last of it, — all Indian River would know of it.

Not a hundred yards away from me, the bear stopped. He sniffed carefully along the sand, followed a trail he seemed to have found along the beach to the dry sand near the bank, and commenced to dig. He worked industriously, scooping the sand out with his paws, and sending it flying over him in a shower. In watching him my excitement somewhat lessened. To be sure, there was still the same danger of discovery as before; but the bear seemed so unconcerned that I could not be otherwise than reassured at his indifference. I even caught myself searching in his dark form for the most vulnerable place for a bullet. From time to time I raised myself to fire; but my hands trembled so with eagerness (not unmixed with fear, I confess) that I dared not trust myself. "Not yet," I whispered; "wait till he is engaged in devouring the eggs, then plug him."

HUNTED BY THE BEAR.

His industry was rewarded; for he soon came to a layer of eggs, and then proceeded more cautiously, drawing out one at a time with his huge paws, and laying them on the sand outside the hole. His head and half his body were immersed in the hole, from which he occasionally backed out to get a better foothold and to survey the eggs he had thrown out.

At it he went again, throwing out eggs and sand. Suddenly he stopped and gave a growl, at the same time retreating from the hole. Looking from him up the beach, following the direction his nose was pointing, I saw another black figure approaching, — another bear!

At this I began to be nervous again; for I had laid my plans to dispose of this bear neatly, but to take care of two bears with only one rifle was out of the question. The bear beneath me seemed alarmed also, but only on account of his eggs; he quickly turned to them and commenced to stow them away in a hurry, standing over them with one paw out ready for a blow, and an eye turned over his shoulder, like a greedy pig at a trough.

The oncoming bear seemed to scent plunder in the air; for he soon broke into a trot, lumbering over the sand at a rapid rate. He approached, and seemed disposed to join in the feast, — a disposition that bear number one was inclined to resent, and he turned upon him with a growl and a snap that plainly told number two to go off and dig his own eggs. With such dainties right before his eyes, bear number two very naturally objected to moving on; or rather he wholly ignored number one's presence, and pushed by and seized an egg. Such an infringement of number one's rights provoked him beyond the powers of endurance, and he drew off and hit number two a sounding slap on the nose. Recovering from this, the latter rushed at his adversary with such vigor that he recoiled; but quickly regained his feet, and threw his arms around number two in a fraternal hug that made his bones crack. Wrapped in a close embrace, biting, hugging, they rolled over and over on the sand. The eggs were hopelessly crushed and mixed with sand; but the bears seemed to have forgotten the object for which they were fighting, and now went on for the pleasure of it.

At last they went plump into the hole number one had dug for the eggs. One of them backed out and commenced kicking in sand, as if hoping to bury his foe alive. This the other did not relish, and scrambled out sneezing, made a dash at number one (or number two, I could not tell which, they were so hopelessly mixed), and strove to pitch him into the pit.

Then ensued a struggle of longer duration than the first. They at once changed their tactics, and commenced a sparring-match, using their great paws so skilfully that neither was able to get in a blow at the other.

As yet they had not suspected my presence. But suddenly one dropped on all-fours, ran a few steps, and quickly raised himself, sniffing the air suspiciously. As he stood there with glaring little eyes and foaming jaws, which, when opened, disclosed a red and cavernous throat, I trembled a little at the thought of what he might be able to do to me if we came into close quarters. I had made up my mind what to do while they were fighting: I would shoot the first one offering me a good chance. The opportunity had come; both bears seemed to have dismissed all thoughts of fighting, and were on the *qui vive* for some common enemy. One of them was on his haunches, his forepaws dropped, his head raised as if in the act of listening.

Sighting carefully at a little white spot on his breast, I fired. Then in all haste I withdrew my rifle, extracted the empty shell, and inserted a loaded cartridge. This was done before the smoke had cleared enough to allow me to see the effect of my shot.

It had not been exactly as I had expected. The bear I had fired at had fallen, all in a heap; he hardly kicked. But the other bear, instead of running away as I had hoped and expected he would, had not moved a foot.

He stood as though petrified; only a moment, though. He recovered from his astonishment, and went up and sniffed the fallen bear. Then it seemed to dawn upon him that that was a dangerous locality, and he started down the beach in a hurry. In my exultation, I could not help rising and sending a bullet after him. Foolish act! He at once stopped, looked around, gave a savage bite at his hip where my ball had struck him without disabling, and turned towards me with as much eagerness in his actions as he had before displayed in getting away.

Here was a dilemma! In my haste, in my flurry, I could not get a cartridge into my rifle. He was within twenty yards of me, — the cartridge would not go in: ten yards, — it still stuck; not twenty feet away, and he was pawing at the crumbling bank below me. I was rapidly revolving in my brain where I should fly to, when the cartridge slipped in. Instinctively I snapped the lock, pointed the muzzle, and pulled the trigger. That settled him, and he toppled over just as his claws had grasped a firm support of roots that would have enabled him to gain the bank on which I stood.

The tables now seemed turned. I was master of the field without a scratch. I laughed to myself over my previous fears, and declared I would as soon kill another bear as not.

Two bears in one night! What a hero this would make me! The hunters of the river would respect me more, and address me less patronizingly than heretofore. Two bears with three shots! Two — Here I stopped in my

"TOTING" THE BEAR.

exultant speech, as my eye fell upon the place where the first bear had fallen. He was not there! He was *on the bank*, not many rods below me; and as I discovered him, he broke into a run, not away from me, but after me.

Leaping to the beach, I ran with all the speed I possessed, — exerted every muscle to keep ahead of the brute that, despite his wound, could yet run tremendously. The beach was my race-course; if I had taken to the scrub the bear would have overtaken me in ten minutes. Along the hard sand I ran for life. The bear was gaining. I was tempted to throw aside my rifle, which was a weight to carry, but clung to it, hoping I might gain one precious moment in which to load it. My strength was going, and the bear's, notwithstanding his wound, seemed gaining.

I turned a curve in the beach, and there I saw my companion, not fifty yards away. He was equal to the test, and did not run, but waited. None too soon was he found, — as I reached him, I fell. He darted out. The bear stopped, — balanced himself on his legs a moment to regard this new foe. It was a fatal pause, and gave Jim the opportunity desired. A shot, and all was over. Two bears were ours, — two bears, which we cut up and skinned and "toted" to our camp before the morning fairly dawned.

The Antiquarian was very much provoked with us for leaving him alone all night, but readily forgave us when he saw our game. He did not, indeed, give credence to my story of the shooting, — in truth, I could hardly believe it myself, the events of the night had been so strange and hurried.

It might have been from envy of my good luck that my friend professed to doubt; but there was no gainsaying the evidence, — we had the bears, and Jim gave me the credit of shooting them. That was glory enough for one night; and I was better satisfied, perhaps, than the Antiquarian.

CHAPTER VIII.

GOOD INDIANS AND BAD WHITE MEN.

IT was two o'clock in the morning when we came to anchor opposite the bluff at Fort Pierce, on the western bank of Indian River. Fort Pierce was our destination, — at least, it was the terminus of our sea-journey. As soon as the anchor dropped, we all "turned in" and slept till daybreak.

In the morning, after breakfast, Jim insisted upon carrying us ashore on his back; for the water was shallow for a long distance from the beach. I, the Historian, was the first passenger, and — well, Jim did n't carry any more, for a certain reason. About half-way to shore, as Jim was carrying me "pickback," I felt a sensation of coolness creep over me, and realized that, somehow, the water was climbing up my back. It got higher and higher, and I soon found that Jim (who meant well enough) was sinking in the mud; and I had to get off and wade ashore, after all.

The Antiquarian hooted his approbation of this proceeding, said he did not require any such assistance as that, and, taking off his shoes and stockings, calmly waded to the beach ahead of me. But Jim meant well enough; only he had found the place in which we had hidden the whiskey bottle.

The trading-post at Fort Pierce was to have been placed at our disposition; but the man in charge wanted a day to move out, and so we waited, not removing anything from our boats. About midnight a small boat came off to us stealthily, and the boatman in it awoke us with the startling intelligence that a murder had been committed ashore, and we were needed to join the force of residents who were going out to hunt up the murderers.

Jim (who had finished his interview with the whiskey bottle, and was just sufficiently intoxicated to feel more valiant than discreet) insisted on taking my best rifle, and going off into the woods at once and alone. But I per-

"AS SOON AS THE ANCHOR DROPPED WE ALL TURNED IN."

suaded him to wait till morning, and he went to sleep; and when morning came he thought better of it.

The circumstances attending the murder were these: Two young men ("crackers") named Drawdy and Paggett came up to the cabin of a Mr. Lang, a German, who had started a nursery some miles from the lagoon, in the pine woods. After taking dinner with him, they requested him to set them across the creek in his boat. He complied, taking them over the creek, about an eighth of a mile from his house; and at about the time he should have landed them, his wife (at the house) heard the report of firearms, since which he hadn't been seen. That was two days before our arrival,

AN OKECHOBEE INDIAN.

but his distracted wife had just got to the lagoon with the news as we reached Fort Pierce. There were very few people in this section, the sheriff was nearly one hundred miles away, and it really looked — as one of the men who brought the news declared — as if there were no law in this county at all.

We were all much excited. Everybody said it was outrageous, and that something should be done; but nobody was ready to take the lead, and so the murderers went at liberty, defying the law.

During the day we got everything ashore and safely housed in a small shanty of two rooms, one of which we occupied (temporarily) and the other was in possession of a negro family of six persons.

The ultimate object of the expedition, it will be remembered, was the rediscovery and exploration of Lake Okechobee, — the largest lake in the South, yet the least known. Two years before, I had tried to reach its shores by land, but had failed on account of having no boat in which to navigate the creeks leading into it. This time, however, I was prepared for all contingencies, and the only thing to discover was a practicable route across country over which to transport the boat. Nobody knew anything of the trail, and it was necessary for me to make a preliminary exploration.

As good fortune would have it, the day after our arrival a party of Okechobee Indians came in to trade. They were of the family of Osceola, deceased, — the mother of Charley Osceola (with whom I had hunted two years previously), and three small brothers. The old lady was very wrinkled, but fat and active; the boys very small, but also active and vigorous.

Upon my expressing a wish to see Charley, Mrs. Osceola said, "Ah ne hiepas-j!" ("Come along with us!") I needed no second invitation; and an hour later was ready, with knapsack, into which I had packed some hard tack, condensed coffee, and pork; a blanket over my shoulders, a canteen filled with coffee, a revolver and knife in my belt, and a rifle in my hand.

We — that is, Sally Osceola, Billy, Jimmy, and Jarneky — then said good-by to my partner, the Antiquarian, and trudged over the sand-hills into the pine forest. Late in the afternoon we reached the only cabin on the trail, the house said to contain the men who had shot Mr. Lang. There was nothing to do but to stop there awhile, as the trail led right by their garden, though our camping-place for the night was four miles beyond.

The owner of the cabin, Jernigan, I had known two years before, when he had led me off into the forests with the intention (as I afterwards believed) of losing me there and appropriating my "plunder." He was an evil-appearing man, with a black-looking face half hidden by a rusty beard, and always carried a gun over his arm. He hailed me with apparent joy, and introduced me to young Drawdy, one of the suspected murderers, — a simple-looking, not ill-favored young man.

While I was drying my clothing — for I had forded a creek a mile above — this young man came into the house and got his gun, drawing out the buckshot, seventeen in number, from the barrel, and then firing off the powder. *The other barrel was empty!* The significance of this lies in the fact that with this gun he had shot the German, and had not reloaded it since, as was later proved, when he was captured.

Jernigan tried to make himself agreeable, and was eager for news from the lagoon, saying he had heard that Mrs. Lang was at Fort Pierce trying to get a posse out to search for the slayers of her husband. He was anxious to know if anything would be done, and particularly inquired if Mr. Stewart, the sheriff, had arrived. He said that he didn't know much about Mr. Lang, but had heard that he was a mighty bad man. "They do 'low round here," he explained, "thet he hed been taken with *heart disease*, and crawled off and died. It's a right smart suddin disease, is heart disease, and persons has often been tuk with it, specially sich as Lang, which shoots our cattle when they feel like it."

THE MURDERERS' CABIN.

It was apparent that he knew something of the murder, if he had not been concerned in it; and I thought that my best policy (at least for the time being) was a non-committal one. I realized that I had unsuspiciously stepped into a nest of serpents, and heartily wished myself back at Indian River. But it would not do to recede, and so I went on with my Indian friends.

At Ten-mile Creek, four miles beyond, the sun went down as Billy was making our camp-fire. He built it Indian fashion with the sticks and logs end together, radiating from a common centre, like the spokes of a wheel, first kindling a blaze by means of dry palmetto fans.

By the time the squaw and pickaninnies had arrived I had prepared coffee and hard-tack toast for us all; the packs were then opened, tin dippers and dried meat were produced, and we "fell to" heartily at the supper. They were easily satisfied, and did not complain at the small allowance I was compelled to give them.

For an hour or two after dark I sat up, questioning them about Indian ways of life, and adding many Seminole words to my vocabulary; then spreading my rubber blanket on the ground, and rolling myself in my overcoat, I went to sleep. Whenever I awoke, I had only to kick the charred logs together to kindle a flame; this being one of the manifest advantages of a fire built Indian-fashion.

At daylight, Billy started a flame by throwing on fresh fuel. I again produced coffee and crackers, and they some slabs of dried meat, which they warmed by hanging on sticks before the fire; and soon breakfast was disposed of, the packs were made up, and we were off on the trail.

Jimmy and Billy tried in vain to spear some fish in the creek, the Alpatiokee, with a spearing-pole they found in the bushes, and hid again when they left.

We passed through the pine woods, and then had a long stretch of wading over the submerged prairie, which lasted nearly all day. The only trees here were the gray cypresses, which grew in "knolls," surrounded by water, and were the abode of hundreds of heron, ibis, and teal.

We reached a strip of pine land at night, and there made a camp as before. In the morning I awoke refreshed, and but little the worse for my tramp except for a slight stiffness; and after a hearty breakfast we took the direct trail for the Indian village, which we reached that night.

What I found there, will be narrated in the next chapter; let us retrace my trail now, in order to finish my account of the doings of Jernigan and his crew.

It was nearly a week later when, having finished my exploration of the country to be traversed with the boat, I returned to Indian River. I had a guide to a point within twenty miles of the lagoon, and thence went on alone, as the trail was well marked, though nearly ten miles of the distance was under water, through which I waded half knee-deep. At about mid-afternoon I reached Alpattiokee Creek, where we had first camped, and arrived at Jernigan's cabin "an hour by sun," or just before sunset.

Jernigan and all the men were out hunting, his wife said; but she gave me a good supper, and then, in spite of her earnest appeals to stay till her husband's return, I went on towards the coast. It was then seven miles to the

THE CAMP IN THE PINE WOODS.

lagoon. Two miles beyond was Five-mile Creek, which was a very bad piece of water to cross, and I wished to get to the other side of it before dark. So I was walking swiftly on, at the very top of my speed, and had almost reached it, when I heard a whistle near me. Looking around, I saw Jernigan and Drawdy approaching, on horseback; while two other men could be seen slinking off into the distant woods. They said they had been out hunting; but they were heavily armed, and came from the direction of St. Lucie Prong, where stood the dwelling of Mr. Lang! They rode close up to me, and urged me to go back with them to the cabin. I held my rifle carelessly in the hollow of my arm, but it was quite ready for action in case of any suspicious movement on their part; and so I stood, half at bay, while they seemed to be making up their minds what course to pursue.

Jernigan was the man I wished to engage to take my boat across country to Lake Okeechobee, as he had the only oxen and cart-wheels in this section of the country. He was very willing to do it, as I made him a liberal offer, but was afraid to go into Fort Pierce to get the boat. If I would meet him at the creek, he would engage to carry my party the whole distance. This I could not do, and finally he agreed to go in for the boat in ten days' time, as he first had " right smart of planting to do;" but I was to treat him squarely, and not say anything to his hurt, for he had heard " how them Indian River fellers spicioned " him and his partners of the Lang affair.

Then I said good-by, and pushed on again, as they turned about and made towards their cabin. It was then quite late, and night was already spreading its gloom over the swamps as I reached the hammock bordering the creek, and walked over the slender poles across it in fear and trembling. Ah! but it was gloomy above that deep alligator hole, into which a single misstep would have plunged me!

It was fairly dark as I waded the "branch" struck across the marshy plain, and pushed on into the woods. Just before darkness obstructed the view, I glanced back, and saw something that made my blood tingle with anticipatory danger. I saw the four men I had left behind me circling to right and left, — two on each side, as if to flank my course and head me off before I could reach the lagoon.

Nothing has since occurred to justify me in the surmise that they intended to cut off my retreat and put me out of the way, as one possessing dangerous information against them, except some dark hints from Jernigan, two weeks later, that I nearly lost the "number of my mess" that night.

It was said to be but four miles from the creek to the fort; but I found them long and weary ones that night, as I strode along in the darkness, my shoes and clothing saturated with water from the mud-holes into which I occasionally plunged. Pool after pool, and marsh after marsh, I waded through, guided only by the glimmer of the water. How anxiously I looked forward to my arrival on the sand-ridge that should show me that the coast was near!

It does not matter now, that the men I saw circling about in the forest did not succeed; I then thought the chances were good for them to overtake me, and then — For an hour and a half I pictured to myself my fate should such an event have come to pass.

At last I ploughed through the loose sand that indicated the proximity of the coast-ridge, and a little later reached the crest and saw the moon, half an hour high, shining brightly in the sky. It was the most grateful sight of that week, except perhaps the light streaming through the window of the house where my partner was quartered. The rest I got there in our half-room was very welcome, and not less grateful was the sense of security surrounding me.

The people at the Fort had collected quite a number of facts regarding the murder, forming indeed a perfect chain of circumstantial evidence against the two Drawdys and Paggett, with Old Jernigan as accomplice. The sheriff had been here, but was afraid to act, as Jernigan and his friends were reported strongly intrenched in their cabin and had threatened to shoot every man coming out to arrest them.

To complete this episode (which occurred several years ago), let me insert an extract from a Florida newspaper of two years later, which was sent me while absent from home in the West Indies. Jernigan had often said to me that he would never be taken alive, and it seems by this account that it was no idle boast. The following is the extract: —

"LANG WAS A SHREWD GERMAN."

"A MURDERER KILLED. — Information has been received from Fort Thompson, Manatee County, saying that Elias Jernigan, one of the murderers of O. A. Lang, was killed near that place on the 18th of January, by a posse who were attempting to arrest him. The facts in relation to the murder of Mr. Lang are written by Mr. C. S. Williams, and published in the 'Union.' Mr. Williams, in the course of a long sojourn in the

Indian River country, became acquainted, we believe, with Mr. Lang, who, in some respects, was an odd genius. He says: 'Mr. O. A. Lang was a shrewd German gardener, educated and accomplished in his business, and well versed in botany and other scientific studies. He came to this country about ten years since, and some eight years ago settled with his family on Lake Worth, Dade County, Florida. Here he lived a solitary life, having no neighbors nor associates, except a few "beach-combers," or "wreckers," and some straggling Seminoles; introducing foreign plants and cultivating vegetables and fruits about six years. He it was who opened the communication between the Atlantic Ocean and Lake Worth, since become noted as the subject of a claim by W. H. Gleason under his contract with the State for ditching. — Gleason claiming that Lang did it in his employ. While living here, Lang made careful and thoroughly scientific examinations of the fauna and flora of that section, and prepared several books of preserved foliage as specimens, with botanical descriptions attached. Wearied of his monotonous life, he removed to a location on the St. Lucie River, some twenty miles or more from its mouth, where he established a home, and finally secured a title to a tract of land, part of which was on an island in the river, and there he made a clearing, and planted various tropical fruits, etc., but for some reason he acquired the enmity of his neighbors — if families living several miles distant can be called neighbors, and it was reported that he was in the habit of shooting their hogs and cattle. Whether this was true or not, or whether it was but a pretext for getting rid of him, is uncertain, but one morning, about two years since, two men came to his house, pretending to be hunting horses. They were known to him, living not far away, and he took them in to breakfast, gave them such information as he could, and finally put them across the river in his boat, when they shot and killed him, — his wife distinctly hearing the shots. His body was sunk in the river, but it rose after a few days and was cut in pieces by the murderers, and the parts stuffed into alligator holes. Subsequent developments revealed the fact that four men were connected with the murder, of whom the Jernigan above-mentioned was one. Some were arrested, and one is now in prison for the crime; the others left the country. Mrs. Lang, with her two or three children, abandoned their plantation, and is said to be living with relatives near New Smyrna. The improvements have gone to ruin, although sugar-cane, bananas, and other fruits are growing there, to be gathered only by wandering Indians or stray hunters. For several years Lang kept a diary, which is said to be in the possession of a resident of Indian River, and contains much that would be of value to citizens and fruit-growers if it were published."

CHAPTER IX

TEN DAYS WITH THE SEMINOLES.

SO jealously do the Seminoles hold themselves in seclusion, that their existence is regarded by many writers as purely mythical. Of the thousands of people who annually visit Florida, not ten get a glimpse of the swarthy red-man.

Along the waters of the St. John's, the mighty river which the Seminole once held as his own, are the winter-resorts of hundreds who little suspect, as they pass the forest-covered fields and mounds which the Indian once owned and cultivated, that the descendants of the aboriginal inhabitants yet live in the State. Far down in the swampy Everglades, a ruined and degraded people eke out a bare existence upon a tithe of the lands which their ancestors once claimed by right of conquest. Few Northern men have ever visited them, so well have they covered the trails to their hiding-places.

No tribe — or remnant of a nation, rather — has preserved its blood so free from contamination as this. No tribe has so sacredly guarded its customs and dress from innovation as this. Despite the changes and rude shocks which the war must have occasioned, the Seminoles have retained their old-time habits of speech, ceremonies, dress, and traditionary rites of religion. They have adopted the dress and habits of the white man only to such a degree as will benefit them, but they cling to the primitive style of garb and speech that their chiefs and old women strove so zealously to preserve in the early part of the last century. They are, therefore, more interesting as a tribe than any other in the United States.

During the late war they maintained a strictly neutral position, though often approached with propositions that they should fight the Yankees. It is possible that they may break the bonds of caution that now restrain them, and dig up the hatchet so long buried; for they are subject to many persecutions by the white settlers who have penetrated into the unattractive Indian reserve.

The Indian settlement near Lake Okeechobee is about thirty miles from the Indian River, upon the Atlantic coast. Between the coast and the settlement, at the time of my first visit, there was but one white man's cabin, and this was some ten miles inland. From that cabin, one April morning, emerged the settler aforesaid and myself.

We mounted two tough stallions, and turned their heads westward. My guide was owner of several hundred head of cattle, which roamed in a half-wild state through the woods and over the prairies, and these horses we were astride were especially trained for hunting those wiry cattle, and admirably fitted for our purpose. We each carried a gun, a pint-cup, and a knife, and across our horses' backs were thrown two well-filled saddle-bags of provender for man, and two more of corn for beast.

A narrow trail led across the vast Alpattiokee Flats, following dry creek-beds, through cypress-swamps and saw-grass jungles, beneath gigantic pines, and through dense palmetto-shrub. We followed this Indian trail in a southwesterly direction, till we struck the saw-grass bordering the Black Cypress, — a cypress belt of swamp nearly forty miles in length, but scarcely a mile in width. Through this swamp was a narrow, blind trail, carefully hidden, lest the white man should discover it.

OSCEOLA, CHIEF OF THE SEMINOLES.

The precautions the Seminoles had taken to guard it were useless; for my guide had trailed Indians in that very swamp years before, and it was to him as plain as noonday. Dismounting, we attempted to lead our horses through it. Bleeding and torn we emerged from the saw-grass, whose serrated edges had cut and gashed us, to enter the blackest swamp that ever defiled the face of Nature. The tall cypress grew high above our heads, excluding every ray

"THE DESPERATE LEAPS OF OUR FRIGHTENED HORSES."

of light. Long trailing vines, and hooked, cruel-looking briers, hung athwart our path, and festooned every tree. The mud in which we struggled was black, and exceedingly soft and tenacious. Stagnant pools of slime-covered water gave lurking-places to numberless alligators and poisonous snakes, which latter reptiles untwisted themselves in dozens from the gnarled cypress-roots, and wriggled silently away after darting at us their forked tongues. It required the utmost vigilance to elude the snakes and the alligators, so as to guide the desperate leaps of our frightened horses.

"HIS PLANTATION WAS A MILE AWAY, IN THE CYPRESS HAMMOCK."

Never was daylight hailed more joyfully than by us at the moment we emerged from the swamp, and dragged our mud-covered horses out upon the solid ground. The Black Cypress was passed; a few miles over level prairie, and we saw the first habitation. This, then, was the Indian country, the last refuge of a persecuted tribe, — these half-dozen miles of prairie, bounded north and east by the swamp, south and west by forests of pines.

The scene before me was one of peaceful rest and happiness. The meadow-lark trilled his clear note from the grass as we rode along; the quail whistled merrily, and the woodpecker tapped the aged pine. Paroquets flew by on golden wings, and the mysterious ibis winged his silent way overhead.

As we neared the village the entire population came forth to meet us; for those at work in the hammocks had been apprised of our arrival, and were there to greet us.

The shanties were grouped together, about thirty in number. They were simply constructed; four posts supported a pitched roof thatched with palmetto-leaves. Open at the sides and ends, a full view of the interior could be obtained. A raised platform of logs, three feet from the ground, was used to sleep upon, and hold the family treasures.

The people that surrounded us were strange in appearance, but the women were most noticeable. Around their necks they wore a profusion of beads, — coil upon coil of great glass beads. They would omit any portion of their attire sooner than these beads, which are of all colors, shapes, and sizes, and the accumulations of years. So long as there is space between the chin and breast, so long do they crowd in beads until the weight is burdensome. Some of these strings have been weighed, and turned the scale at twenty pounds. They are slaves to fashion, — these untutored sisters. The only exception to the general style of dress was in the case of a young widow, who, according to the fixed and unalterable laws of the tribe, was permitted to wear no beads, no cape, no bustle, or polonaise. The law regarding widows is, furthermore, that they shall not leave camp for two years, nor comb their luxuriant hair during that period. If they pass the time of probation with credit, they may marry again.

To summarize in respect to dress: Children of both sexes under five cavorted about in a state of nature. The boys enjoyed this freedom, unrestrained, until ten or twelve years old; but the children of the softer sex donned a petticoat. At fifteen the boys arrived at the dignity of a shirt. The girls of that age had accumulated vast possessions of beads, and when turned sixteen were allowed to wear a cape.

Upon great occasions both men and women ornament themselves regardless of expense. The men disguise themselves in shirts of fine make, and long, flowing gowns of large-figured calico, embroidered elaborately and belted at the waist. Their legs are encased in fringed leggings, and their moccasins are shapely and highly ornamented. Around their heads they wind a large, gayly colored shawl, making a huge turban, from which the fringe hangs gracefully. Heron and egret plumes are thrust into the hair, and from the neck are suspended large gorgets of silver. The women use a profusion of ribbons, bracelets, and beads. About their ankles they tie shells of the box-tortoise, which are bored with holes, so that they make a loud noise when struck together. They manufacture ear-rings from silver half- and quarter- dollars, without any instruments for working save the most primitive. These observations I made while surrounded by the motley crowd, and during my subsequent residence with them.

After a short rest, we were invited by Indian Parker, a sub-chief, to inspect his plantation. It was a mile away in the cypress hammock. Their houses are built in the pine-woods for health, while their gardens are in the more fertile, swampy hammocks.

His wife and children were hard at work when we arrived, but desisted at the first intimation of visitors, washed themselves in a creek, donned their clothing, and gathered about us with offerings of the fruit of the place,— corn and sweet-potatoes. The corn we roasted in the ashes, and ate the great milky ears with much satisfaction, though our sleeves did not brush away all of the clinging dirt.

It was in April; and Parker had corn six feet high, and pumpkins, beans, peas, and melons, in flourishing growth. All worked,— men, women, and children. There were no shirks. This is a pleasing characteristic of the Seminole. He will hunt all the time that he can be spared from his plantation; but when the season of planting comes, the rifle and arrow are laid aside, and he takes up the hoe and axe. Labor is mutual. The warrior kills the deer and bear, skins it, prepares the meat, and brings it home or to camp. The squaw, sister, or daughter dries and dresses the skin, smokes the meat for future use, and performs all the labor incident to the camp.

From Parker's plantation we went beyond, to that of Tiger, his father-in-law. I had met Tiger two weeks previously. He had visited my camp and eaten me out of provisions. At the time of his visit I had enough food, with the game we shot, to last three weeks. He came with ten younger men, stopped with me over-night, and left me next day without a pound of flour or meat in the larder.

"THE NEXT DAY THE PERFORMANCE BEGAN."

My guide had attended the annual feast of the harvest, or "busk," the previous year, and described to me this interesting ceremony:—

"'T was about the fust of July, and Aleck and me thought we 'd go out and kind of celebrate the Fourth among the Injuns. They give us a shanty, and we turned our hosses loose, and the next day the performance began. You see that cleared place thar, about a hundred feet across? Well, that was all smooth, and was used to dance on, around that thar pole, which was hung with leaves, and one sort of thing and another. This house, here to one side, was a sort of sweat-house, and they had it stopped up tight, and a big kettle of water — two or three of them — in one end.

"The women, they went round and collected all the old stuff and made a big heap of it, and then set it afire. Then they went out and got some kind of a root and made a strong drink; and that physicked them, you bet. This took about all day.

"Next day they got together on that level place, and danced about the pole. They did n't like it because we was there, and some of the Big Cypress fellows threatened to kill us; but Aleck had brought out a keg of real good whiskey, and the promise of that, when they was through, made everything all right.

"The women had them turtle-shells strapped around their ankles, and they 'd clap 'em together and make a noise you could hear a mile. First they 'd dance kind of slow, then gradually quicken their steps till they would fairly wake things, and sing and howl fit to wake the dead. All these two days they had n't had nothing to eat, and would n't give us anything; and if we had n't brought something, we should have starved.

"Every once in a while one of the chiefs would get up and make a speech, and then dive into the sweat-house, where they had got up steam by chucking red-hot rocks into them kettles of water. There he would stay till nigh about dead, — for the house was all full of steam, — and then he 'd rush out and jump into that pond there, stark naked, and yelling like sixty!

"All this time the old doctor seemed to be the master of ceremonies, and he was a-mumbling over big words, hard enough to choke a white man, and pretended he was conversing with the Great Spirit. Toward night of the second day they seemed to think they 'd got things about clean enough, with their sweating and physicking and dancing, and all the girls went off and got corn and melons and pertaters, and they had a reg'lar feast, and they eat and eat, till everybody had enough to make up for a two months' fast.

"This is all the ceremony these heathen have, and they don't care no more for religion than a cat. If they are good when they are on this earth, they will go to a land of plenty, where things is cheap and whiskey and game is plenty. If they don't be good here, they will go to the land of the Bad Spirit, who is half starved, and has no bear's-oil or whiskey. After the ceremonies was all over, they elected old Tustenuggu chief, instead of Tiger-Tail, who has been chief so long, and that came near making a fight; but it was proved that Tustenuggu was descended from old Micanopy, and had ought to have been chief long ago."

Giving a last look to our horses, we retired to sleep upon the hard logs, awoke early the next morning, bade adieu to our kind friends, and departed, intending to return in a few days.

Of the week that followed, — of our being lost in the woods, and finally emerging at the settlement we sought, — I will say nothing, for that had nothing to do with the Indians.

When we returned we found the shanties deserted. Not a living being was within sight or sound. Carefully stowed away beneath the thatch were deer-skins, tortoise-shells, and small household articles. In one shanty we found a rifle and a spelling-book.

We were out of provisions, and must find some Indians or starve. Starting for their plantations, darkness gathered about us before we could find the trail through the swamps. Wheeling the horses about, we galloped over broad stretches of prairie toward the trail through the Black Cypress; for that way the trail led, and we felt sure we should eventually overtake them. The moon came up and flooded the prairies. We passed a group of deserted dwellings, and were greeted by the hoot of *oopah* (owls) from their bare ridge-poles.

Soon we entered the gloom of the Cypress, where scarcely a moonbeam could penetrate, and struggled for an hour in the horrible blackness, with the terrors of our previous passage increased tenfold by the darkness. Exhausted, we led our horses out into the moonlight, mounted and rode on, soon striking the prairie upon the other side. The trail of the Indians was fresh, and my guide followed it without difficulty. On and on we rode; the outlines of the cypress, curved and beautiful, melting away in the distance. Halting to give our jaded beasts a bite of grass, we mounted again, anon falling in with herds of cattle and giving chase.

The monotonous, long-drawn cry of wolves wailed out faintly on the air. My guide assured me that there was nothing to be feared from them, as well I knew; yet that cry caused me to grasp my rifle tighter and look back over my shoulder more than once. Another wail, nearer now, and another answering, gave promise of good watchmen, in case we had to camp alone. Our horses pricked up their ears at the sound, and pressed forward with renewed

"THE GLOOM OF THE CYPRESS."

speed. A long spell of silence, broken only by the thud of hoofs, ensued, worse in its suspense than the noise of the wolves.

"They are on our track!" said my guide, "but I don't know what it means. I ain't seen a wolf on this prairie this year, and there's either a big pack after us, or a starved one." We entered the shadow of a palmetto-grove, and dashed over the cracking fans as though we heard the wolves on our track. At the farther end we halted just a minute. Patter, patter, — I seemed to hear the noise of many feet, and urged my horse on, while a cold thrill ran down my back.

In the midst of a heavy canter we saw the gleam of lights at our right, heard the barking of dogs, and wheeling about soon found ourselves in the midst of friends. A host of dogs came forth to meet us, and leaped about and frolicked just as white men's dogs would do. As we crashed into the hammock over dead and brittle limbs and leaves, a sleepy Indian greeted us, who assigned a place for us to sleep, and roused a drowsy squaw, who set out various vessels of food and then retired.

Kicking the embers of their camp-fire together, a blaze leaps up that brings out the weird features of the scene. Lofty palmettos, with imbricated trunks, stand out gray and ghastly, supporting an arching roof of broad leaves, beneath which, singly and in groups, are stretched the sleeping Seminoles. Many strange objects loom up, and familiar things take unfamiliar shapes; but we are too tired to analyze the picture, and only too grateful to stretch our weary limbs beneath the palms, safe in the company of friends.

It was long past midnight when we had finished our attack upon the meat, sausage, and "thin drink;" and the sun looked in upon us several hours before we awoke next morning.

An Indian camp is this village, moved into the forest, *minus* the houses. Nearly all their personal property is carried with them. Hogs, dogs, hens, cooking-utensils, and every other movable thing, is taken with them when they set out on a grand hunt. This party was destined for the prairies of the St. John's, intending to be gone a month and procure hundreds of deer-skins. They marched by easy stages, and hunted as they went. They were to stop here a few days, to kill a couple of bears in the cypress-swamps near; then they would move on.

Tied to a tree near my head was a half-grown bear, who lunged at me fearfully as I arose and threw off my blanket. Two small pigs were tied by the middle to another tree, and through all the day they raised their pitiful voices to heaven for deliverance. A litter of puppies, with eyes yet unopened, snarled and whined beneath the shade of a palmetto. Upon poles, stretched from tree to tree, were piles of deer-skins, and large bear-hides curiously stretched with sticks and thongs. From the trees hung pots and kettles, spoons, dippers, blankets, bladders, bottles, fawn-skins of honey, deer's brains wrapped in moss, leggings, saddles, saddle-bags, bear-meat in huge flakes, axes, knives, and thongs, and as miscellaneous and varied a wardrobe of feminine garments as ever adorned an Indian camp.

After breakfast, the squaws and girls busied themselves with the various employments left them by their husbands and fathers. One dressed skins; another prepared bread from the powdered *contikatke*, coontee, or breadroot; while the little ones ran about, stark naked saving their beads, gleaning the fragments left from breakfast, inverting themselves in the huge kettles in search of some choice morsel, or licking the bowl of some huge spoon.

I never tired of watching their antics. They were as cheerful and as jolly as white children, and carried on their games with as much gusto. They never cry. There was a babe there but three weeks old, laid out on the palmetto fans, which never even whimpered. They made curious little shelters of palmetto leaves for the children. The stalks of some of these leaves are three feet long, and the leaves as much in diameter; and these would be thrust into the ground, the leaves joined at the top, forming a charming little tent, turning rain and dew, and allowing free play for the wind between the stalk-supports.

The process of dressing the deer-skins is interesting. The skins are fleshed, thrown into water until the hair peels off readily, then thrown over a post sunken into the ground at an angle of about forty-five degrees, rubbed till perfectly smooth with a piece of wood, and then smoked. This smoking process colors them, in shades varying from yellow to brown, makes them comparatively waterproof, and gives them a villanous odor of smoke, which is retained as long as the skin exists. To smoke them, they dig a small pit, build a fire at the bottom, place upon the fire pieces of rotten wood, and over the pit place the skins, which have been previously softened with a mixture of deer's brains in water. After smoking, the skins are hung up to dry, and are ready for market.

Toward noon one of the girls led the surly bear-cub to a neighboring pond to drink. He walked by her side peaceably enough until he got opposite us, when he darted so fiercely in our direction that the thong that held him parted. Forgetting the peculiarly ursine predisposition to climb, so inherent in a bear, I started up the nearest tree. It was smooth. A dozen feet from the ground I hung, unable to proceed. It was a desperate situation. Below was a raging bear, sharpening his claws in bloody anticipation; above, the smooth bole of the tree, slippery as glass. I ask the reader, What would you have done? Verily, nothing different from what I was doing, — digging toes and finger-nails into that miserable tree. But there is a limit to human endurance. My arms weakened, legs shook, muscles quivered. One desperate effort — I was gone! So was the bear! After playfully scratching at the root of the tree awhile, he allowed himself to be caught and led away. Not being aware of that, I had hung to that tree full fifteen minutes after his departure. I never did love bears.

Late in the afternoon a handsome squaw came in from the swamps with a huge load of brier-roots. Without vouchsafing a word to any one, she deposited her load on the ground, procured water, washed a kettleful carefully, and then placed them in another kettle half filled with water. This she hung over the fire, packed a thick layer of Spanish moss over the top, and placed over this a strip of the inner fibre of the palmetto; all this was done to keep in the steam. A few hours' steaming over a slow fire was sufficient; they were taken from the kettle, mashed to a pulp, strained in several waters, dried, and then reduced to a fine flour. This was the *ah-há*, or China brier, by some called the wild potato. This and the coontee furnish the Seminoles with an abundance of farinaceous food. It is of a brick-red color; the powder of the coontee-root is of the color and appearance of rye-flour. The squaws baked thin cakes of it, and gave them to us, served up in honey. The honey found in these woods is delicious, made mostly from the wild pennyroyal. The Indians are exceedingly fond of it, and spot a bee-tree a long way off. They carry it in fawn-skins, said skins being stripped from the

"IT WAS A DESPERATE SITUATION."

animals nearly whole, stretched out till dried, when, with the nose tied up, they make water-tight bags.

At an hour before sunset we heard the report of a gun, then another. That was all; but the squaws looked at one another, and said, "No ko-sé" (Bear), and busied themselves in preparing a repast for the hunters and putting the kettles in order for trying out the oil.

A little after dusk the braves came in. First came villanous-looking but honest and pleasant Parker and his son, each loaded down with bear-meat; and behind them Parker's son-in-law, bearing a portion of meat and a huge hide.

Old Billy came next, the most perfect specimen of an old Indian I have met. He was tall, with brawny limbs, a large Roman nose, and large eyes. Tommy Tiger, a Spanish Indian, followed after him, threw his meat at the feet of his squaw, and stood upright, with folded arms, eying us savagely. Tommy Tiger was a son of old Tiger. He was over six feet in height, large and muscular. His eyes were black and fierce; his mouth, firm, but not cruel, was shaded by a small black mustache. We soon made friends with him, and found him gentle and pleasant-voiced.

Every one was now full of activity; the squaws took the bear-meat and venison, cut the former into small slices, which they strung upon sticks to smoke, and trimmed the hams of the latter. The brave's work for the day was done. He had procured the meat and skins; the squaw was to prepare and preserve them.

Though wet, weary, and hungry, they were very kind and courteous, answering quietly the questions of the children as they clung to their legs and hands, while at the same time conversing with us.

And this has been my experience with the Seminole. I have found him ever kind, hospitable, generous, and brave; worthy a better fate than is before him. So long, however, as he is left alone, he asks nothing more. He is happy. The forests and rivers furnish food in abundance; and if the native Floridian does not extend his encroachments farther, the Seminole will continue to live in peace and harmony with mankind, asking nothing, needing nothing.

We remained with them several days; and, were this but a tale of adventure, I might prolong it many a page; but my only aim has been to represent the Seminole as he is in these pictures of camp and village life, and enough has been written to show the manner in which he lives.

"IMPENETRABLE SWAMP AND GLOOMY FOREST."

CHAPTER X.

LAKE OKECHOBEE.

FAR down in the Everglades, in the unknown interior of Florida, surrounded by impenetrable swamps and gloomy forests, lies the mysterious lake of the South, — the vast Okechobee.

When its existence was first made known to white men history does not affirm; but if one were to choose to believe that an intimation of it was conveyed to the gallant De Leon in the oft-related story of the chimerical "Fountain of Youth," — restorer of health and rejuvenator of the aged, — he would seemingly have support in historical facts. It is related that De Leon received his information from a Carib maiden, — one of a tribe then inhabiting the Florida Everglades, the Keys, and the adjoining islands. He landed, it is said, upon Cape Sable, the southernmost point of land in Florida, and penetrated northerly in the direction of the lake.

The traditions of the earlier tribes of Indians were few. Respecting their origin, the country from which they came to Florida, they knew little. Their traditions related principally to tales of wonderful hunting-grounds and waters. If, like the later tribes occupying their lands, their legends referred to the Great Lake, it is more than probable that those "Indian sages," met with by the old soldier Ponce de Leon, had this in their minds when they said (accepting the poet's rendering), —

> "The leafy Bimini,
> An island of grottos and bowers,
> Is there; and a wonderful fountain
> Upsprings from its gardens of flowers."

Either this rendering or the Indian, De Leon or the poet, was imposed upon. But if we cannot claim for the Great Lake that the fact of its existence was imparted to white men in 1512, we can bring forward historical data to prove that its presence was not unknown a few years later, in 1539, when Ferdinand de Soto first landed upon the coast of Florida.

Then the discoverer of the Mississippi was told that the province in which he landed was called Macaco; that the ruling cacique, or chief, bore the same title, and that the great source of supply of the various rivers flowing into the Gulf of Mexico was known by that name. By this name, Macaco, as well as by that of Mayaco, Lake Okechobee is known to the older writers. We may deduce from these facts that the possibility of there being a large body of water in the unexplored interior was intimated to Europeans more than three centuries ago. To the Indians of the interior it was the symbol of the Infinite; and doubtless they worshipped it, and the sun that arose above its far eastern horizon.

They regarded with veneration the largest body of water known to them, excepting the ocean; and this may account for the universal manner in which, from first to last — from swarthy Yemassee to olive Seminole — they have hidden it from the search of their white brother. Its vastness filled them with awe; and, unable to explore it in their frail canoes, they called upon the imagination to supply what they could not discover. Thus it was the paradise of the red man — his happy hunting-ground on earth. Thus was the lake dotted with wondrously beautiful islands, and the far shores of white and glittering sand bordered a land of crystal fountains, beautiful birds, and flowers.

To this lake has been attributed the source of the St. John's, the wonderful river of Florida. When Aviles descended the St. John's, many years ago, he was told that the river had its rise "in a great lake called Miami, thirty leagues in extent, from which streams also flowed westerly to Carlos" (Carlosahatchee River). A learned writer remarks: "Lake Mayaimi is identical with Lake Okechobee, called on older maps, and, indeed, so late as Turner's and Cary's, Mayaco and Macaco."

The ancient geographers represented water in the southern interior of the peninsula; so it seems that they must have been better informed than later ones, who have omitted the lake entirely. From evidences in various portions of the adjoining country, it would appear that the early Spaniards were more thoroughly informed of the lake than their successors.

Lake Okechobee has had a great reputation as being the chief source of supply whence the enormous quantities of pearls once possessed by the natives were obtained. Mention is made of a certain Spanish governor who despatched a successful expedition to the Great Lake for these precious substances. Whether this lake was the seat of the pearl-fisheries whence came

ON THE ST. JOHN'S.

the supplies of the natives, from whom De Soto and his soldiers took away bushels, will not be argued; but certain it is that they were obtained from a source now exhausted or unknown. The only mention of the lake in the last century is by Romans, who in 1772 relates the story of a Spaniard taken captive by the Indians and carried by them to the shore of the lake. He escaped, and returned with wonderful tales of the region he had penetrated.

The Seminoles have a tradition that the first white man ever seen by their ancestors was upon the shore of this lake. He came out of the sea, they said, and then disappeared. It may have been the same captive whose adventures were related a hundred years ago.

At the commencement of the present century the lake was as little known as at the time of De Soto, and it was not until the necessities of war demanded the search of the Everglades, forty years later, for our enemies, the Seminoles, that any definite knowledge regarding it was obtained. Until that time, as stated by a writer of that period, "the interior of this part of the Territory was wholly unexplored by white men, and the description of the Indian inhabitants was at best imperfect. When I explored the coast, my force was not sufficient to ascend the large rivers that enter the Gulf of Mexico, and the great lakes that are believed to supply these rivers are *wholly unknown*." During the protracted Seminole War of 1836–1843 the lake was crossed once or twice. In the later war, 1856–1858, more accurate information was obtained of the northern portion of its shores, and two military stations were located near its borders, — one west, the other east of the lake. But notwithstanding the frequent visitation of its northern shores during the war, upon the withdrawal of the troops all communication with the lake ceased, and it returned to the seclusion its past history had awarded it. Since that time it has remained wholly forgotten until recently, — except, perhaps, by the few hundred Indians living in a half-wild state in the Everglades. These Seminoles have steadily repulsed and discouraged all attempts at its exploration, for reasons important to them, perhaps, but unknown. From time to time have appeared sensational stories of the wonders of Lake Okeechobee. Ruins of castles and monasteries, with carved and ornamented pillars; ruins of Indian cities; dens of pirates, containing untold treasure, — were found upon an island somewhere in the Great Lake. Indeed, some ubiquitous party had explored the lake, and had found monkeys and baboons, — whether on land or in the glassy water they had seen them, no one knows; and delightful groves of tropical fruits decked beautiful islands, and everything was charming and serene, and everybody wanted to take the first boat for Okeechobee! Ruins they had found also, and islands with breezy bluffs and grassy plains. They had seen — O horror! — "spiders of four pounds' weight!"

Such was Okeechobee when I first undertook its exploration, which proved a failure. Nothing was definitely known; everything partook of that vagueness and was tinged with that romance which such a mysterious body of water in a section of country unknown and unexplored for years, surrounded by Indians alleged to be hostile to white men, and swamps heretofore impassable, was likely to create. But the semi-tropical lake was not forgotten, especially when the blasts of winter came; and now I was once more on Indian River, fully prepared, by the experience of my previous misadventures, for a thorough exploration of the lake.

Though I had undertaken the exploration alone and unaided, when the final start was made my party included five persons besides myself and the two drivers. As each one was an active participant in the scenes herein to be described, it is but just that the reader should form their acquaintance. The Professor had come to me recommended by the leading naturalist of America. He was a valuable acquisition, erudite, and companionable. The Doctor, his friend, was an indefatigable collector and naturalist, who had visited nearly every Indian tribe in North and South America, and had had much experience in tropical countries. Two students accompanied them, fresh from college and enthusiastic. But the mighty man of valor was a Dutchman, whom we will call Van Buster, whose only aim in life seemed to be to see new and strange sights and lands, and report thereon. His "corporosity" and visage gave ample credence to his statement, oft reiterated, that he was of Dutch descent; and a subsequent reading of the "History of New York" has satisfied me that his claim of descent from one of the first families of New York is fully substantiated, from a union of two of the most noted clans, — the "Van Houters, of Kaatskill, most horrible quaffers of new cider and arrant braggers in their liquor;" and the "Van Kortlandts, much spoken of for their skill in shooting with the long-bow." Thus it will be seen that our party was eminently respectable, and competent to undertake a complete exposition of the fauna and flora of southern Florida.

VAN BUSTER.

Leaving the party assembled at the river, I departed for the interior in search of a team for the transportation of my boat across the country. The man[1] whom I had selected as guide was an old "trailer" during the Seminole War, who owned a little cabin ten miles from the coast, half a thousand head of cattle, and a few horses. He was ready to go, but had no wheels; and we visited a neighboring "Cracker" who had just arrived, to solicit his.

As a Cracker, typical of the species, a slight sketch of him and his establishment will be given. The two carts, simply rough boxes of pine plank, were mounted upon hard-pine axles and very shaky wheels. Over the top were drawn strips of thin cotton over arched hickory-poles. They were a very feeble imitation of the Western immigrant wagon. In the carts was the entire collection of domestic utensils and furniture, including several hide-bottom chairs, a spinning-wheel, a cradle, a rough pine table and hominy-mill, which nearly filled them. Astern of each cart was lashed a rough-slab hencoop.

Two yoke of diminutive steers were quietly grazing a little way off; the hens were seeking food about the camp, and some half-dozen children were playing about the cart.

The wife of the Cracker, his "old woman," was busy cooking hominy in an iron pot suspended from a pine limb, smoking a cob pipe the while, and contorting her pasty face fearfully in vain attempts to make the "blamed thing dror."

We saluted the Cracker. His name was Pigpen. "Good-evening, Mr. Pigpen!"

"How d'ye, gen'lemen?"

"I want them wheels of yourn a few days."

"Well, I reck'n you ken hev 'em."

"How much will they stan'?"

"Well, I 'low as how they'll stan' right smart, — reck'n they'll stan' twelve hundred poun's."

"Are you sure?" I interposed.

"Heap sartin; they'se brung all them traps from Manatee, an' my old woman 'lows they'se more 'n twelve hundred poun's to the keert."

This individual desired to make a favorable impression, and informed us that he had a "hundred head uv hens an' a heap uv cattle in Manatee."

"Do the hens all roost in the coops?"

"Well, no; kinder squats round permiskus."

Other information of a kindred nature did he vouchsafe, but I quickly closed a bargain with Jernigan, the cattle-hunter, and rejoined my party. At

---

[1] Jernigan, mentioned in a preceding chapter.

the appointed time (noon, of February 14th), Jernigan appeared with his assistant and team of two yoke of steers.

We were awaiting his arrival; and after an hour or two spent in fitting the axles to my boat and disposing of dinner, we loaded the boat with the articles each considered necessary. Besides our provisions of pork, hard-tack, hominy, and coffee, of which each had ample supply, there were many things. The Doctor and Professor had large cans of alcohol, bales of paper for plants, cans of arsenic for birds and beasts, fish-nets, insect-nets, etc. A huge knapsack of tin, weighing fifty pounds, containing every known appliance for capturing, preserving, and transfixing every living, creeping, crawling, walking, flying, swimming thing upon the face of the earth, the water upon and beneath it, and the circumambient atmosphere, the Professor proposed carrying upon his shoulders, but we labored with him successfully not to do so. The students had other knapsacks, a hundred pounds of powder and shot, and vast stores of arsenic for the preservation of birds. For myself, there was a trunk of chemicals, and provision, ammunition, etc. The camera and necessary chemicals were for procuring pictures of the ruins said to be in the lake, and thus assist in bringing shame and confusion upon those unprincipled persons who dared assert that this nation, this free and enlightened people, "possessed no ruins!" Our armament was complete. We had thirteen deadly weapons to the party. More weapons of destruction were started upon that expedition than had been in the country before since the war.

When all was ready the team was started, and the panting oxen drew the rickety wheels through the loose sand. Slowly they filed out of sight, — the diminutive oxen; the swearing drivers; the Colonel (with this sobriquet the people of the river honored Van Buster), to whom I had yielded my claim to the only horse; the Professor and students, looking for birds; the Doctor, seeking bugs.

Half an hour later when I walked to the brow of the sand-ridge with my partner, who was to keep camp, there was no one in sight.

"Good-by, old fellow; I'll be back in a month!"

"Good-by! Send a note back by Jernigan!"

Then I trudged down the hill, across the marsh and into the pine woods, leaving behind me the truest-hearted fellow in all Florida.

The sketch of our route was something as follows: It was called sixty miles to the Kissinee, a river supposed to flow into Lake Okechobee. My boat was to be transported overland to that river, where it was to be launched, and we were to descend and explore the lake. There is an old military road crossing the peninsula from the Atlantic to the Gulf, which crosses the Kissinee, but at a point farther north than another, — an Indian trail, which I had chosen. This latter was but knee-deep in water on the average, while the other was neck-deep even swimming. We were to keep the trail for about twenty-five miles, then strike across the prairies of the head-waters of the St. John's, travel a few miles on the old military trail, and then cross the Kissimee Prairie southwest.

Four miles out, I discovered the party assembled about the boat bewailing a broken wheel. Though all despatch was used, it was two days before that accident was repaired, and during that time we camped in the pine-woods. A new set of wheels was procured with difficulty, and the boat was reloaded and the old wheels left in their tracks, where they remained five weeks later upon our return.

The first deep water encountered, Five-mile Creek, was swimming, — that is, so deep that neither oxen nor wheels could touch bottom. The leading yoke was taken off, swam across, and the team entered. Our driver stripped naked, and one of the students and myself did likewise. With a shout from all hands, the steers plunged into the stream with Miley, the driver, at their heads, where he swam at the risk of being gored in their wild plunges, and Shores and myself swimming astern to guide the boat as it struck the bank. As soon as the wheels struck bottom and the steers had gained footing, they refused to move. It was a critical moment; for the current, though not swift, was gradually raising the boat from the wheels, which were sinking in the quicksand. There was no time for delay, as the sand was slowly, surely, creeping up the spokes. The leaders were hitched on, and amid the plaudits of the Colonel and the Professor, who stood on the bank aiding us with encouraging smiles and advice, the boat was drawn from the creek, and our team stood panting and dripping upon the bank. This creek is formed by the converging of the waters that, miles above, spread over the flats and prairies of the St. John's.

Four miles farther is Jernigan's cabin, where we halted, and where we parted with much regret from the Professor, who afterward reached the lake by a different route. The road to Ten-mile Creek was "right-smart palmeetery," — rough palmetto-roots causing the alcohol-cans, chemicals, etc., to dance in a lively manner. We reached and crossed the creek without serious delay, and camped upon its western bank at noon, beneath a huge oak. Here we caught a few large black bass, which had been left in small pools by the drying of the creek, and took a refreshing bath.

After a short rest we marched on, striking the Alligator Flats just beyond the creek. These flats are miles in extent, submerged over half the year. At Trout Creek we struck a curious formation of cypress-clumps. They are in rounded knolls, and stretch away in every direction, resembling in appearance the Holyoke Mountain of Massachusetts, as seen from Springfield.

The mud and water grew deeper and deeper, and as far as we could see was one stretch of water, dotted with cypress-clumps. The poor oxen tugged and strained, yet moved but slowly through the mud, nearly axle-deep, through which we on foot plodded wearily, half knee-deep in its miry depths.

FLATS AND PRAIRIES OF THE ST. JOHN'S.

Occasionally we started a moccason-snake from the grass; and many times did we tread near them, barely missing their heads. These snakes are deadly poisonous, as much to be dreaded as the terrible rattlesnake. Lurking in the tussocks of grass, and concealed beneath the water, they are more to be dreaded than the rattlesnake, which generally gives warning before it strikes. These, however, give no warning, but swiftly and surely strike their envenomed fangs deep into the leg ere the traveller is aware of their presence.

Toward night I walked ahead of my companions, with orders for the team to meet me at the Indian camp, in a pine-island in the swamp. At dusk I reached the camp, and finding a convenient log of pine-wood left by the Indians, started a blaze for the guidance of my fellow-travellers. Soon they came in, one by one, wet and tired, and dropped by the fire. After the oxen were turned out to feed, Miley baked potatoes, barbecued meat, and cooked hominy, the water being obtained from a cypress-pond near by, where the snakes writhe and twist among the cypress-roots, and where the frogs hold noisy concert all night long. After an hour's talk over the fire we "turned in" and slept profoundly till morning, when we arose at daybreak, and started an hour or two later.

It was but a repetition of the day before, except that there was more prairie with deeper marsh, where we waded knee-deep in the swampy mire, with the snakes wriggling among the small bushes and grass-roots in close proximity to our feet. I have not mentioned that the Doctor, Shores, the student, and myself were barefoot most of the time, and any anxiety may be attributed to our disinclination to come in contact with a snake; for a snake always does feel cold and clammy when touched by the naked skin, and we do not like to give our nervous system such a shock as must inevitably ensue. We kept an eye open for snakes.

We travelled for miles over a broad prairie, across which we could see a line of cypress; around us, and occasionally surrounding us, was a dense marsh.

"Yonder's a 'gator, boys!" said Jernigan. We all made a rush for him, and soon were grouped about an eight-foot alligator, high and dry on the prairie. He made no attempt to escape, as he was perfectly well aware that all efforts would be perfectly useless, and received our shots without a motion; hardly a groan escaped him. As it was the first alligator Shores had encountered, to him was awarded the privilege of shooting him.

We pushed on, till noon found us at the largest cypress-clumps and spurs of a beautiful rounded outline, conspicuous from their isolated positions, called the "Blue Mountains." Here we took a long nooning, as the oxen were nearly famished. The grass was short and sweet, as the prairie had been recently burned over.

South of us, ten miles, was the Seminole town, and about twenty miles southwest, Lake Okeechobee; though, from the character of the country intervening, we were obliged to treble that distance.

A slight shower passed over without wetting us much, and we travelled on till nearly dark, crossing Cow Creek and an old trail once used by the soldiers in passing from Fort Loyd to the Kissinee River. At Cow Creek we struck the St. John's prairies, in no wise different from the others, except that they extend far to the north to Lake Washington, the extreme head of navigation on the St. John's.

At dark we reached "Cow-bone Camp," where is a clump of palms and grass for our cattle. The place received its name from the bleaching skeletons of cattle, the accumulation of years, which were strewed around.

"Many's the bull-fight I've had here," said Jernigan; "and many's the bull we've had to kill before we could go on with the branding."

Multitudes of cranes dotted the prairie and marsh, and turkeys were occasionally seen; but our numbers precluded a successful approach and capture. Deer were seen at times; but the Seminole had hunted here for a generation, and this made them scarce and shy.

It was late next morning before we started, as the cattle were lost in the marsh; but after finding them we forced our way through a "cypress-slue," where the mud was axle-deep and the cypress-knees thickly strewed, and emerged upon a clear, open prairie, where we could see ahead for miles. North and east was the broad prairie, dotted with pine and palmetto; south and west, a line of cypress-swamp, extending for forty miles. After crossing this prairie we entered a wood of pines, and emerged from that upon the old military trail, where every tree was blazed, and not a tree or stump obstructed.

Three miles over this trail brought us to a deserted house, where once lived a well-to-do settler. One of the distinctive characteristics of a Cracker is his unrest. He rarely stays half a dozen years in the same place, but wanders from county to county, seeking the promised land of Crackerdom, — a land flowing with corn and whiskey, hog-meat and hominy. He will settle at a new place upon the slightest provocation; perhaps there is promise of a good cattle-range, or a "right smart chance" to grow corn or potatoes; then stops the team, the cattle are turned out to graze, and a log or palmetto shanty goes up in a jiffy. Upon equally slight grounds will he vacate the premises. If the fleas get uncomfortably thick, if a panther kills a few calves, or if the proprietor hears of a better land, away he goes, and the house and clearing are left desolate. So now, where I found thrift and apparent prosperity two years ago, I found a home deserted and a wilderness. A flock of wild-turkeys were feeding in the cleared field; and as I was ahead of the party, I had an excellent opportunity to secure one.

Wild-turkeys are excellent barbecued, with just the right proportion of fat pork to baste them, and our driver was just the man that could do it well. He could barbecue a turkey so nicely as to make one's mouth water after a hearty dinner. Mine watered. I concluded to have that gobbler, the leader of the flock, and drew my Remington revolver, which had never failed me, and fired. The turkeys looked up in astonishment, but soon resumed their feeding. Bang! The bullet ploughed the earth at their feet, but the one nearest where it struck merely hopped up and resumed his search for food. This was provoking. I never had such shooting before. The next shot winged the gobbler, and the way those turkeys " dusted " was astonishing.

Three miles farther is the site of old Fort Dunn, with nothing to indicate it except the old parade-ground, covered with a younger growth of pines. Here we crossed Fort Dunn Creek, the ultimate head-water of the St. John's River.

"Do you remember that cypress-bulk down yonder?" said Jernigan.

Ah! well I remembered that dark-green clump; for that was the first landmark known to my guide when we were lost two years ago. There commenced the most southern affluent of the mighty St. John's. At the same place "headed" another creek, taking a different direction southwardly, into the St. Lucie Sound and Indian River; reaching the Atlantic coast two hundred miles south of the waters of its brother creek, flowing into the St. John's. The creek at the crossing, two miles north, is very shallow, but in the wet season very broad. We camped in the pine-woods near the Kissinee Prairie that night, and our horse and cattle luxuriated upon the fresh grass of a recent "burn."

At sunset we saw the sun go down upon the Kissinee Prairie, and gild with its last rays the blue cypress-swamp containing the fountain-heads of two of Florida's largest rivers. At one o'clock next morning, Jernigan aroused us, and we soon had the coffee boiled and a hasty breakfast disposed of. We then started, for we were determined to reach the river before night. We had twenty miles farther to go, having accomplished forty. The darkness was intense, and it was wonderful how Jernigan, walking ahead, could discover the trail.

Soon we left the old road, and struck a narrow trail leading southwest. A dense fog hung over the land, but we pushed on, with our guide ahead; and no sound broke the stillness, save the crack of the driver's whip and his occasional shout to the cattle. For an hour we went steadily on, and I closed my eyes and yielded myself to the drowsy influence stealing over me. But something soon caused me to sit upright with a start and rub my eyes. The wind, which had fanned my left cheek as I lay down, now blew directly upon my right. While I was striving to account for this phenomenon, the team came to a sudden halt, the driver uttered an exclamation, and he and Jernigan held a consultation in low tones. We had missed the trail. In the darkness and fog we were as wholly lost as a ship at sea without a compass. We go farther to the north and strike a marsh, in which we bog. Extricated from this, we turn south, and are lost in a wilderness of reeds. We have had the wind from all quarters, and are completely at loss as to our course.

Jernigan then seized the horse and started off in a circuit about the boat. We whooped at intervals to guide him in the darkness, and anxiously awaited a response. Minutes seemed hours as they glided by, with no answering cry. Then there came a cry, — the long, shrill whoop of the cattle-hunter, — faint in the distance. Turning our cattle that way, we sought, and after a long search found our guide. Lighting some dry grass, we found unmistakable evidence in the worn soil and smooth palmetto-roots of the trail. Not long after, the first gray of morning appeared; and it seems that we had been lost for hours, for we could see the woods we left far in the distance. The eastern sky slowly brightened, and the sun came out and dissipated the mists.

An hour after daylight we passed a cypress-swamp, where rises the famous Taylor's Creek, which runs into Lake Okeechobee, upon the banks of which General Zachary Taylor fought one of the hardest battles of the Seminole War. The slope of the prairie is unmistakably west, toward the Kissinee River. We saw what looked like a river, but what, in reality, was only fog. The illusion produced by the fog was complete, and we saw houses, gardens, and cattle, which another mile of distance resolved into mist. Occasional bunches of cattle, a few sand-hill cranes, and a few herds of deer bounding over the scrub-palmettos, were the only living objects we saw. Nearing a belt of pines, fifteen miles from our starting-point, we saw unmistakably a house. The trail leads through a swamp and then into the pine-woods, by this log-cabin. This proved to be the residence of Henry Parker, a large cattle-owner, who had made this wild place his home to avail himself of the size and excellence of the cattle-range; for, with his brothers, he was owner of twenty thousand head of cattle, which were shipped to Cuba from the Gulf coast, as the market required.

From Parker's to the Kissinee is about five miles, — three through rough pine-woods, half a mile over prairies, and a mile and a half of wading, then the Kissinee River, deep and dark, though narrow. Alligators grunted at us from the reeds, coots and gallinules swarmed in clouds before us, and the ibis and snake-birds covered every shrub. There was just dry land enough upon the river-bank to unload the boat upon; which done, we launched her, put in all the luggage, sent the team back to the pine-woods, and rowed rapidly down-stream to the western bank. Here, at the ford, we found high, dry banks, and a good camping-place. Two small water-oaks mark the ford on the western bank, and some rotten cattle-pens, in the swamp, the eastern. The land is covered with a dense growth of scrub and water oak, back of which is a broad stretch of pines and prairie. The road from Manatee to the Atlantic coast crosses here. Above is a marsh of lilies, willows, and reeds, and marsh below. A mile south is the site of old Fort Bassenger, where General Taylor crossed, marching to subsequent defeat, at the battle of Okeechobee.

The Kissinee River rises far north, in a succession of lakes, and flows, for

HERONS.

two hundred miles and more, with tortuous course, southward into Lake Okechobee. The upper waters are beautifully diversified with islands; and the country through which the river flows is covered with oaks and pines, affording shelter to numerous flocks of turkeys and herds of deer.

The southern portion, however, flows through a marshy region, with little game, and few localities suitable for hunting. Throughout its whole course it is narrow, and extremely crooked. At the ford its width is about fifty yards, though, at high seasons, it spreads over the adjoining country for miles. The current is swift; the water dark, cool, and sweet. No one knew the distance to the lake, and there had been but three white men there for fifteen years.

We camped at the ford two days, waiting the arrival of Mr. Parker with a "beef." Here the Doctor came near being drowned, and would have been had it not been for the gallant efforts of Shores, who, though the unfortunate cause of the mishap, nobly atoned for all by his prompt rescue. The 22d of February, being the Sabbath, should have been devoted to its proper use as a day of rest; but that being impossible, from the superabundance of mosquitoes, and the nearest place of worship we were cognizant of being three hundred miles away, we did the next best thing,— got our boat loaded and started for the lake.

The air was balmy, and vocal with the songs of birds. We rowed easily down the stream, between banks of water-lettuce and yellow lilies, passing still lagoons where coots, gallinules, and water-turkeys swam and dived and chattered, in blissful ignorance of guns and hunters.

The river makes a grand sweep not far from Fort Bassenger, and we boxed the compass in a course of three miles. A flock of hundreds of white ibis flew before us for miles; the sun, glinting their glossy backs and black-tipped wings, produced a beautiful effect.

Alligators were not numerous, preferring those sections of the river where low shelving banks or projecting sand-bars give them sunning-places. The shore preserved its marshy character as we proceeded; occasionally a water-worn bluff made up to the shore, covered with a wilderness of trees and tangled underbrush.

Ten miles down we discovered a rookery of white herons. Their large nests, built of sticks, a foot and a half across, were placed in low bushes, just above the water. Each nest contained two large, greenish-blue eggs. We secured a couple of dozen in a few minutes, and pushed on, promising to call again upon our return.

A few miles farther a rifle-shot of ours provoked an answering bark. Rounding a live-oak bluff of unusual thickness, we saw two boys and a pack of dogs standing beneath a large oak. We brought our boat to anchor near a palmetto-thatched shanty, and there soon appeared a white woman and a negro wench.

We learned that this clearing was the property of Thomas Doughtery,—a Tennessean by birth, a Floridian by adoption. He had moved here from Fort Dunn because "varmints was powerful bad thar," and he couldn't raise good corn. This bluff was formerly the property of a Seminole, of whom Mr. Doughtery bought it. The Indian shanty was still there, and we visited an old Indian field and inspected a corn-crib of Indian workmanship, rat-proof and water-tight. The Doctor said it was exactly similar to those now in use in the Choctaw and Seminole nations west. Upon the logs of his shanty was stretched a large panther-skin, that had been taken from an animal killed near our camp of the night before.

Giving some fish-hooks and lines to the boys, we cast off, and drifted down the stream.

This was the last white man's residence we should see for several weeks. No one had passed their bluff since their arrival but a family of Indians a few days before. A mile or two farther we discovered a small hut, made of palmetto-leaves, evidently the work of the Indian family ahead of us. We stopped here to dine and give the Doctor rest, for the heat was intense. A sweep in the river soon hid the hut from our sight, and we rowed between tree-fringed banks, with very low shores, where opportunities for landing were few indeed. A pine-ridge on our left seemed to approach the river, but did not reach it, and nothing broke the monotonous swamp-line; and night approached, with no prospect of a camp. At last one of the numerous curves disclosed a large maple upon a high bank. The place was instantly seized upon for a camp; the boat was brought about, and, secured in an eddy, lay safe for the night. A fire was started at the roots of a fallen tree, and ran through the dead wood and grass to kill vermin and start out the snakes. The bank is narrow, but large enough for a fire and sleeping-place, and we stretched our canvas and turned in, after a good supper of bass, caught on our way down. A pine-dotted prairie is seen back of us, with a mile of swamp intervening.

Casting off bow and stern lines in the morning, we floated between banks overhung with maples and occasional palmettos. Coming to a place where the river forked, and beds of water-lettuce and masses of canes made choice, of course, very difficult, we let the boat drift, taking the stronger current. Then we came to a glimpse of prairie, where pines and palmettos diversified the plain. A sudden turn to the left revealed an aged oak,—lone sentinel in this vast swamp, its trunk and broad limbs clothed in a dense covering of long gray moss. Upon its trunk were cut the letters "F. L. S." and "J. C." I climbed the oak and looked off. Before me, south, lay the river, — a bright stretch of water for a mile, then suddenly lost in the marsh. Far away to the east I could see two large cypress-bulks, seemingly the terminal points of the pine-ridge which had followed the course of the river several miles away; west, a palmetto-ridge came down, sweeping away far westward. Between these two ridges was a vast plain, with here and there a single tree. Beyond that, I felt —

"SOON THE RIVER RESUMED ITS CROOKED COURSE."

I could not see — was Okechobee; for the line of the horizon seemed beyond the line of plain. Quiet lagoons opened out here and there, where the trees and bushes were white with the nests of the snake-bird. Numerous as are these birds upon the St. John's and the Ocklawaha, they were in tenfold numbers here. The most abundant bird was the odd crying-bird, — the limpkin, courlan, or Indian hen. Everywhere we saw it, jumping from the grass at every turn, rending the air with its cries.

Soon the river resumed its crooked course, narrowing to less than twenty yards across, which width it held to the end. No pen can describe its crookedness. Twisting, turning, doubling on our course, we rowed between banks of saw-grass and reeds, and marshes of canes so high that they overtopped our heads as we stood upon the rail of the boat. It was depressing in the extreme, and we grew weary long before night came on. Just before sunset we discerned a lone cypress, — a broad-topped, well-formed tree, with branches reaching to the ground. It was covered with snake-birds, which flew away silently at our approach. The bow of the boat touched the shore, and I sprang into the tree and climbed to its very top. Turning about, I saw at last the long-sought lake, the *ultima Thule* of our hopes, Okeechobee, — a faint-blue line; upon the east, a darker line of cypress; west, an immense plain.

Darkness prevented us from staying, and we had but a moment to peer through the glass, which the Colonel brought up, before descending. By the faint light of the stars and the new moon, we sought the channel, rowing in the shadow of the trees, and finally emerged into what seemed a broad bay, where a gentle swell rocked uneasily, and we could hear the murmuring of waves. In the darkness we concluded it was not safe to go farther, and accordingly threw the anchor over, and drifted to leeward of an old cypress. Mosquitoes attacked us. Fury! how they bit! This was our welcome to Okeechobee, — our first reception, — music by the band! We retired beneath our bars, where we might listen to the soothing strains unmolested.

This was our first night aboard the boat. As but one of several nights thus spent, it will answer as a description of all. The Colonel and myself slept aft. There was space there, four feet by three. We squeezed ourselves into that space, drew the bar over us, and essayed to sleep. The knees of the boat were troublesome, and we used, in lieu of feathers to soften the bed, sundry boots, bags of shot, and bits of broken wood. The Doctor stretched out on a thwart, six feet long and a foot wide. He did not sleep well. He had not yet recovered from the terrible shock at Fort Bassenger. Shores had, for his exclusive use, the cracker-barrel. For the first time in his life he was heard to utter the wish that barrels were longer and curved the other way.

An old cormorant flew around me many times as I lashed an oar to the tree, next morning, for a landmark. He seemed anxious to obtain, for the benefit of his friends, a good description of the first white man he had ever seen.

The bay formed at the entrance of the Kissinee into Lake Okeechobee is a mile in length from east to west, and half a mile in breadth. It is nearly filled with yellow lily-pads and the floating water-lettuce, though the line of the marshy shore may be easily traced. East is a large body of cypress; west, a smaller clump; between, north, is interminable marsh. The blue waves dance in the sun, and I could see nothing to the south but water, — far away south to the horizon-line.

A heavy swell came in from the lake; but we rowed out into the open water, and sought a landing upon the western shore. Cypress, dead and white, against which the waves dash violently, stand far out in the lake. Cautiously we forced our way through them, and made a happy discovery. Back of the phalanx of cypress-knees is a little drift of yellow sand, — merely a drift, such a ripple as a huge wave throws up in a moment, and wastes away again; but it seemed a very paradise to us, this sand-bar with its overhanging maples and ash, intertwined with huge grape-vines and hung with moss. Landing, we built a fire and cooked a much-needed breakfast. We spent nearly half a day here, drying our provisions and investigating the flora and fauna of our little island.

In the marsh behind it was a black lagoon, whose still surface was crossed and recrossed by huge alligators. The Colonel and Shores shot at them, laying low many a one. The Doctor unearthed many an innocent bug, and deposited a few new specimens of plants between his sheets of bibulous paper.

The wind rose, and our sand-bar proved a poor place for the night's camp. Skirting the cypress, we scanned the shore for a landing-place; none appeared. A few miles west, a sand-bar gleamed out behind the cypress; but no sloping beach appeared upon which we could run our boat, and the water was full of cypress-knees, which threatened destruction to it. While my companions held her in position, head on to the rollers, I jumped into the water, waded ashore, and sought a place to land; found a narrow passage leading by a land-locked lagoon, and through this we ran the boat, and hauled her up, secure against wind and waves. We found indications of an old camp; and the charred logs, with the ends together, radiating from the centre, proclaimed it to be an Indian camp. Availing ourselves of a large log cut by our unknown friends, we soon had a fire started and supper cooked.

The Doctor and myself were the self-elected cooks, as Shores was unwell, and the Colonel was too lazy to do aught but smoke and talk. We had appetites like wolves, and rapidly and ravenously devoured hominy, pork, and beef.

Our old friend the crying-bird, with whom we had got acquainted on the Kissimee, paid us a visit, and cackled and shrieked for our benefit all night long.

From this point we could trace the eastern shore — a line of trees — till lost in a deep bay. The western shore runs southwesterly, and is mostly marsh.

The wind was ahead. We could not sail; and the Doctor and myself took the oars and rowed all the forenoon toward what appeared to be an earth-mound, but which a near approach resolved into clumps of reeds. A deep grass bay sends an arm into the marsh, and a few grass-shoals loom up in the water, like islands afar off.

CHAPTER XI.

MORE ABOUT LAKE OKECHOBEE.

IN a little bay, separated from the lake by a fringe of grass, we tied up to a cypress-tree, and started a fire upon some cypress-knees, where had lodged a foot or so of earth. The water of the lake is so thick with organic matter that we could not drink it unless boiled with coffee, and so a fire was necessary every time we took a drink. Shores made a fire; the Doctor put in the coffee while I held the pot over the flame; and the Colonel descended the tree just in time to get a drink and escape an attack from a swarm of carpenter-bees, who had neatly chiselled holes in every limb of the cypress.

In the afternoon we rowed on, striving to reach a dense cypress-point; but toward night a sudden squall came on, blackening the water and sending rippling masses scurrying over the surface, and we hurriedly ran the boat through a bank of grass and reeds to the still waters of a quiet lagoon, where a noisome stench proclaimed decaying vegetation.

Our old friends the mosquitoes renewed acquaintance, and seemed desirous to watch with us through the night; but we bade them good-night, and turned in. Sleeping in the boat was rather difficult at first. Doubtless there are softer feathers than old boots and bags of shot; but the Colonel and myself occupied the bed in the stern, while the Doctor and Shores covered, respectively, the thwart and cracker-barrel. From various and sundry kicks and snorts, which came to my wakeful ears during the night, I judged that the mosquitoes were doing what they considered their duty.

At daylight we crept out into the lake, gladly leaving the black pool to the alligators and snakes. The wind was from the north, and we sped along, under double-reefed sail, beneath a sky of inky darkness. The cypress were reached

THE CAMP ON THE ISLAND.

after sailing through a narrow channel between floating vine-covered islands and a broad grass-shoal.

But what a disappointment awaited us! Instead of the land for fire and rest, we found floating islands, the trees surrounded by water and densely matted together with vines. The tall cypress rose far overhead, and many lay floating on the water; but there was no land. Throwing the anchor over a fal'en tree, we started a fire upon its dry roots and boiled our coffee.

Pushing our way through stunted cypress, causing the snake-birds and cormorants nesting there to rise in clouds, we finally reached a beautiful hammock, where, back of the water-line of cypress, could be seen the delicate foliage of the maple. We ran the boat upon the sand and stepped out. Stiff and cramped with our long confinement on board the boat, we hailed with joy this opportunity to stretch our limbs.

The narrow ridge was densely covered with a growth of cypress, maple, ash, India-rubber, boxwood, and mulberry. Here upon a box-tree, in whose trunk was cut an inscription in large characters, we found signs of the former occupation of this island. We gathered about this tree, and speculated what the characters were meant to represent,—

(J. Smith 1^{000}_{873}).

"I have it," said the Colonel; and when the Colonel said he had it, we all listened attentively,—"I have it. These characters were made by some of them Norsemen we read about coming over here eight hundred years ago! See! 1000, the year they came here; 873, the number of the men. This name, here, was that of one of their chiefs."

"But," said the Doctor, "that can't be; the bark would have covered the inscription, and the tree would have decayed hundreds of years ago."

"That may be; but couldn't this be a young tree,—a sucker grown up from the roots of the old one?"

"I think the Colonel's the sucker," said Shores.

I connected this inscription with a story told me before we left the ford, of one John Smith, who essayed to find Fish-eating Creek, who was lost, went three days without food, and would have perished but for timely discovery by a band of Indians.

The most noticeable feature here was a gigantic cypress, six feet in diameter, enveloped in a mesh-work of wood,—the trunk of the parasitical fig, or "India-rubber." Towering aloft a hundred feet, wrapped in the close embrace of the parasite, wound about with vines whose leaves rivalled in color our Northern maple in autumn, the feathery foliage of the cypress blending with the glossy leaves of the rubber made a charming picture of tropical beauty and luxuriance.

The nests of the osprey were everywhere; and as his enemy, the white-headed eagle, does not live here, it seems as though Mr. Fish-hawk might pass his days in peace and happiness.

Our course was southwest. We crossed a deep bay, some five miles across, to examine its farther shore for that creek with the unpronounceable name, — Thlathtopopkahatchee, or Fish-eating Creek. Not that we wished to revel in a feast of fishes, or were actuated by any other desire than to explore the lake. But we dipped into bays, and navigated blind creeks, and threaded sinuous channels, beneath the hot sun of mid-day, and not a glimpse of Thlathtopopkahatchee did we see; and it is our private recorded opinion that, should we have found the mouth of Thlathtopopkahatchee, it would have been rather small, anyway.

Late in the afternoon we reached a small island, — just a hint of sand above the water, — and seized upon the opportunity offered for an attack upon the coffee-pot. The low trees were filled with nests of snake-birds and herons, loaded with eggs and young. The alligators were very numerous and familiar; they would sail slowly up to our boat, rub their noses against it, and manifest an inclination to form our acquaintance, until there were several dozen about us. A few rifle-shots and sundry raps over their snouts would cause them to retire a few yards and gaze at us in a wistful way, truly touching.

The marsh here is intersected by many creeks and bayous, but very few trees appear.

We undertook to cross a bay south of this island, but darkness came on, and a sudden gale of wind lashed the waves into immense billows. We scurried for shelter into a bay in the marsh, and were forced to pass the night there, with a strong force of mosquitoes to keep watch. 'T was a fearful night. Shores and myself were afflicted with a touch of fever, and in the morning he was so sick as to be unable to work.

The south shore stretched away for miles, — the same desolate expanse of marsh, fringed with scrubby willows. In a long stretch of coast but one tree was in sight; and just as we reached that tree, next morning, the wind died away. It was well. Our only mode of observation was by ascending trees, and we should have stopped to climb that tree if the wind had blown a gale. Tall trees were few. Perhaps we had passed a dozen isolated ones, and we had climbed every one. Our feelings were elevated proportionably to our elevation above the level of the lake. The inclination so grew upon us that we were seized with a desire to climb every tree higher than our mast.

From that tree I descried a dim island, and all the weary afternoon we rowed for that island, with the sun shining fiercely upon our blessed skulls. Distance was deceptive on that lake, and it was sunset ere we struck the grass shoal surrounding the island, toward which white wings had been flapping in the distance, and snowy birds had been winging their way. It was dark before we found a landing and ran the boat ashore, on a high, dry sand-ridge, overtopped by ash and India-rubber. As I shouted my discovery to my friends, there was a rustle in the tree-tops. White, ghostly shapes flitted from tree to tree and fluttered overhead. A black snake darted from some wood that I was gathering, and startled me still more. The light of the moon struggled feebly through the leaves; but it was not until I had a rousing fire that I discovered that the island was inhabited, — that the great white heron had nests on every tree.

Two days were devoted to a systematic exploration of the island; for here, if anywhere, in this, the only island at all inhabitable in the lake, should be found those remarkable ruins discovered by those remarkable mythical explorers who claimed to have preceded us.

The only things bearing any resemblance to ruins were the beautiful rounded clumps of the dark-leaved ipomea, — shapes easily transformed into ivy-draped castles and towers.

The centre of the island was covered with huge India-rubber trees, delicately foliaged box, and sweet-scented bay. The eastern or lake shore is a rim of snowy sand, beaten hard by the waves; the western, a dense, tangled mud-swamp, swarming with snakes, alligators, and mosquitoes.

Here grew gigantic ferns, and gorgeous, flaming, epiphytic air-plants. The entire length of the island is about a mile and a half. The northern end terminates in a rank growth of swamp-trees, and is in places covered with wild-gourds and pawpaws in flower and fruit.

Near the southern end is a tall cypress, from which an extensive view of the lake is obtained. From its top I could see the shore north, west, and south; east, all is water. Two islands loom up south, — one a little islet a mile away, the other dim and misty. Southwest I could see a row of palms, and a beautiful glassy lake lifted up into the sky, — a mirage, occasioned, I think, by the presence of some lake miles west of Okechobee; probably the head-waters of the Carlosahatchee, which connects with Okechobee at wet seasons.

Upon a limb of the cypress was cut "T. W., 1857," thus confirming the report that this island was used as a place of *reconnoissance* during the war that drove the Seminole from this his last resort, and made peculiarly applicable the name "Observation Island."

In the afternoon of a pleasant day the Colonel and myself shot a few herons for their plumes. The dark masses of the ipomea were dotted with herons, white as snow, beautiful, graceful, their long plumes waving in the wind. At the first reports of our guns they left the island and their thousand nests to the mercy of those egg-thieves, the fish-crows, who reaped rich harvests. We saw a few of those magnificent birds, the rosy spoon-bills, and found a few of their eggs.

The Colonel shot a huge snake as we entered the swamp, which circumstance deterred him from penetrating very far into its dismal depths; but I, unconscious of the fact, was far in advance, having excellent shooting.

As soon as a heron was killed, I would strip the plume of downy filaments from its back, and throw the body upon the ground, passing on to the next. After coming out of the swamp I heard a report, and then another; and soon appeared the Colonel, very much blown, but jubilant, holding high above his head, out of harm's reach, one of the herons I had shot and stripped.

"I've got one," said he, "a reg'lar stunner; but, by thunder! how I raked his back!"

He would not accept my version of the shooting, but made himself miserable for three successive days and nights in vain endeavor to convince me that "the charge of shot just raked every feather clean off the bird's back."

Our sick man was much refreshed by our stay at this island. The few days had been filled to overflowing by the Doctor in collecting bugs and plants, so that we left it, after a sudden gale had abated, in good spirits.

The dim island, as seen from the cypress, proved to be a mile or so of sand-beach, backed by interminable marsh. Huge cypress covered the beach; down the long vistas are charming views. We call this lonely beach "Fossil Beach," from some rare fossil shells the Doctor finds here. Three deep bays, each some five miles across, terminate Lake Okeechobee at its southern shore. They are lined with the same desolate shores of reeds, canes, and scrubby willows, and the successive points terminate in scraggy "custard-apple" trees, filled with the nests of cormorants and snake-birds.

A lone cypress terminates a long point of marsh, and back of this is a deep bay, the last and southernmost.

Here are the Everglades, where the water of the great lake filters through an immense swamp, through the spongy shores of grass, canes, and lily-roots, through gloomy forests of cypress, to the ocean and the gulf.

No creek, no river, forms the outlet of the waters of this vast lake; the accumulated drainage of thousands of square miles of territory slowly percolates through the Everglades by thousands of channels with countless ramifications. Northwest of the cypress is a chain of partially submerged islands, which we reach one night just at dark, vainly seeking a fragment of *terra firma* sufficiently large to build a fire upon, and casting anchor in a dark pool, peopled only by ibis and alligators.

Our attempts to sleep were ineffectual, as the mosquitoes were cruel and bloodthirsty; and after several hours' battle, we concluded to sail for the eastern shore.

It was midnight. The moonbeams feebly lighted up the dark Everglades; the same moon had accompanied us from our first camp on the Kissimee until now we were looking upon the river for probably the last time. It was a fitting ending to our dreary voyage along the Everglade shore that we should leave the forsaken stretch of marsh and swamp, and enter upon the home-stretch with all the repulsive features softened and chastened by the moonlight.

Farewell, forever, to the Everglades!

A few hours after the wind died away, leaving the water like glass; and we lowered our sail, and anchored opposite the southernmost point of the eastern shore.

Shoals of alligators swarmed up, their black heads dotting the water like water-worn pine-knots. They rubbed their noses against the boat, and grunted loudly and deeply, — a welcome, perhaps, though we viewed it in the light of a welcome addition to their bill of fare. Time and again we shot at them; but neither the death-dealing bullets nor the reports — which reverberated through the swamp like noise of cannon, and started out large flocks of ghostly ibis — alarmed them, and we lay down to rest, secure of a watchful guard throughout the night.

The heat of the sun awoke us next morning, and we pulled for a clump of palms and a snowy beach, where, beneath graceful palms and overarching vines, we stretched our weary limbs. The beach was covered with shells of various hues, fragments of coquina, and nodules of clay. Windrows of mussel-shells with iridescent hues we discovered, but did not find the famous pearl-mussel, which history affirms the Spanish governor of long ago found in such quantities.

As we sped along the shore, we noticed that the trees grew larger, — cypress, ash, and India-rubber, — and we could trace the line of the shore far away to the north.

Late in the afternoon we made a landing. As the keel of the boat grated the sand, an ominous splash greeted us, and the water was covered with bubbles and foam. In explanation of this we saw a huge snake — a moccason, poisonous as death — slowly unwind himself from the upturned roots of a prostrate India-rubber, and glide into the water. Out of the grass and down from the trees they came, — a repulsive, hideous concourse of slimy snakes. We waited until the procession had passed out of sight, and then leaped ashore, determined to camp, snakes or no snakes, as it was nearly dark. The ridge of sand is very narrow, covered with palmetto, boxwood, and rubber trees, and back of it is an impenetrable marsh of saw-grass. A well-beaten alligator-trail led from the lake to a little pool in the edge of the swamp, where the sand had washed over, forming a pure white basin of clear water. From this pool we dipped up water clear and sweet. Oh, how refreshing to our parched lips, after two weeks of the green broth of the lake! In this we found beautiful water-lilies, exactly the counterpart of our Northern *Nymphæa odorata*, but tinted with the hue of yellow topaz.

The next day we found a beautiful bay, with a wide white beach, above which rose large trees, draped with graceful festoons of long gray Spanish moss. The song of the cardinal-bird and the exquisite notes of that inimitable mimic the cat-bird fell gratefully upon our ears. A stiff southeast breeze sent us flying along the shore, and caused the waters of the lake to rise in huge billows that threatened to engulf us as they increased in size. In the afternoon we sought a lee behind a marshy point, only to find that we had entered a deep, narrow bay, down which the wind drew us as fiercely as from the lake. There seemed to be a creek emptying into it, and it is about two miles in depth. It is the bay known upon the old military maps as Cohancy Bay.

Finding no shelter here, we again sailed on, the waves growing heavier and larger, dashing at times clear over us. Several miles farther a white beach gleamed out behind the cypress, and we made a landing after much danger and a complete soaking in the surf. A surprise awaited us. As I ran up the beach with the anchor, I stumbled over a hewed cypress-plank. Looking about, we saw a group of bananas, their broad leaves lashed by the wind. Beyond were the ruins of several palmetto shanties, the corner-posts alone standing, the roofs sunken into the ground. Pawpaws in flower, sugar-cane, and guavas flourished amid a wilderness of swamp-growth. There were boards strewed upon the beach, ten feet in length and a foot in width, hewed by hand. This, the first permanent camp I had seen on the lake, I afterward ascertained was during the Indian war the village of a Seminole chieftain, who now resides in the "Big Cypress," southwest of the lake.

The clearing embraced several acres, but was now so completely overgrown as to be impenetrable. One of the cow-hunters subsequently told me that he had visited it while hunting Indians from the prairies behind it, and was obliged to wade nearly a mile in mud and water. I was upon the prairie back of this swamp in 1872, but could not reach the lake. It is about fifteen miles from the Kissinee. Next morning, the waves having subsided, we launched the boat in time to take the southeast breeze, which rises at about nine every morning, blows through the day, and subsides at sunset. A deep bay, similar to the bay of the Kissinee, deceived us, and we sailed far up it, with a fair wind, and were obliged to row painfully back again, reaching the main shore at dark, when we camped in a dry swamp.

The next morning, as we rowed along the cypress-fringed shore, we saw the strangest sight of all our trip. Upon the shore stood a man, a nomadic Hoosier, "looking at the country." He was tall, well formed, roughly dressed. His boat was a dozen feet in length, a foot high, and built of hard pine,— merely a box. His oars were whittled from pine-slabs. He had a blanket for a sail. A small box contained everything he had else; no gun, rifle, or fish-line. All we could induce him to accept was a box of matches.

Leaving our new-found friend, who had braved the dangers of the lake in his frail skiff, we rowed through the floating islands of lilies and water-lettuce to the cypress at the mouth of the Kissinee. Our voyage up the river was without incident of any note; we reached the ford the third day up, and the Atlantic coast the thirty-third from our departure. In all that time there were but two falls of rain. The average daily temperature was $75°$; the nightly, $50°$ to $55°$.

The lake is about forty-five miles in length, from north to south, and thirty in width, from east to west, near the centre. The distance from the Atlantic to the Kissinee is sixty miles; down the river, fifty-five; and around the lake, at least a hundred. This makes our journey a hundred and twenty miles land-travel; a hundred and ten by the river,— lake and all, over three hundred and thirty miles.

The lake has been for the first time thoroughly explored. Its topography you have examined with me, and its natural history will be made known when our dear friend the Doctor brings to light the contents of his bales of plants and cans and bottles of alcoholic specimens. Until the line of stage and steamer connecting the St. John's with Okeechobee is inaugurated, the tourist desiring to visit a new and in some respects a little-known country cannot do better than take boats and guides for the largest lake in the South, the much-maligned Okeechobee. Taking warning and wisdom from the narration of our misadventures, he may be able to "do" the river with as little discomfort as is practicable in more northern waters.

Our first day of unalloyed happiness was at Judge Parker's, where we engaged horses and means of transportation to the coast. There it was that we stretched our legs beneath a table for the first time in many days. We rehearsed the story of our adventures to an attentive audience, with the Colonel as spokesman. He detailed every circumstance, from the first conception of the enterprise to its fulfilment, with a minuteness that showed profound study and powers of observation. He had saved the Doctor from a watery grave by shouting a talismanic word as he went down. His provisions had kept us from starvation, — in fact, he had been the savior of the party. He incidentally alluded to his descent from one of the oldest families of New York; spoke in glowing terms of the prowess and renown of his valiant progenitors, and modestly affirmed that he was winning a fame that promised to eclipse that of his forefathers, wholly dependent upon his individual effort. Then he recalled a scene in the lake when the whole party was in imminent danger of being drowned by a furious alligator.

Warming with his theme, he grew eloquent, describing the approach of the alligator, his horrid appearance as he rose from the water and climbed into the boat, and the horror of the Doctor as he saw his beloved cans of alcohol and bales of plants disappear down the cavernous throat of the monster as he approached the party, huddled together in the stern of the boat.

"It was at this juncture," said the Colonel, "that I recalled my presence of mind. I was the only one of the party brave enough to face the alligator. The rest sat paralyzed with fear. Fortunately, I was equal to the emergency. I advanced boldly. I seized the alligator by the snout, spit tobacco-juice in his eyes, and while the creature was blindly seeking to strike me, I, by a dexterous movement, seized him by the tail, and —"

What was the *dénouement* no one will ever know, for the Colonel disappeared from our sight. In his excitement he had arisen from the table and taken a few steps into the outer darkness, beyond the light of the blazing pine-knots. Like the puffing out of a candle, he had gone. His voice had ceased.

We looked at one another, rubbed our eyes, and looked at the Judge. He smiled. "Flea-pit!"

To explain: So annoying and plentiful are the fleas that pits, two feet in depth, are dug for the reception of any unwary one that may be skipping about in the exuberance of its spirits. Two pits are generally considered necessary.

From beneath the table came groans and oaths; subsequently appeared a frowsy head and a red face, plentifully besprinkled with sand and little sticks. That sight would have upset the gravity of a graven image. Our sick man exploded and collapsed. The Doctor choked and grew black in the face. I rose to pat him on the back. Tears blinded my eyes, — tears of mirth soon changed to those of genuine sorrow.

As I rose, a hog darted between my legs. He was a tall hog, with the

A MOUNTED WARRIOR.

frame of an elephant, the backbone of a racer. To express it briefly, he was taller than my legs were long. I rode a few feet and then fell off. I felt a shock; my cervical vertebræ seemed driven against the roof of my mouth. The toes of my boots abraded the cuticle from my nose, and it dawned upon me that this was the other flea-pit.

To this day I consider the laughter that greeted my premature exploration wholly uncalled for.

The Doctor, even, laughed himself off his chair, and rolled on the ground, emitting a succession of "Oh dears!" that grew fainter and fainter as his breath grew shorter and shorter.

There is little now to add, for our return journey to the coast over the same old trail was without important incident.

I found my partner, the so-called Antiquarian, anxious over our protracted stay, and happy to see us once more safely with him after the month's absence. His trading had not been so successful as we could have wished, and in another week we had "packed our traps" and were aiming for the head-waters of the St. John's River.

CHAPTER XII.

INDIAN TRADITIONS AND FOLK-LORE.

BEFORE taking final leave of the Indian River country, we lingered awhile for additional information regarding the Seminoles, particularly of those who had bought stores of us and had promised to pay at a certain time.

At exactly the time appointed the party of Seminoles came in, headed by Indian Parker, the honest sub-chief; and as they stayed several days, camping out on the beach, we improved the opportunity to obtain additional words for our vocabulary.

According to Indian Parker, there are now two distinct bands of Seminoles in Florida, sometimes further divided into three or four. The wildest of them all live over in the Big Cypress, on the west side of Lake Okechobee, in a region practically inaccessible. These are direct descendants of the original Creeks, who came into Florida, from the north, about a century ago.

The Okechobee Indians are the wealthiest and have the best land, and contain among them such famous personages as Indian Parker, Micco, Tony, Charley Osceola, Tustenuggee, Billy Smith, and Tommy Tiger.

Away south of Okechobee and Indian River, on the borders of the Everglades, near Key Biscayne, is another collection of Indian families commanded by young Tiger Tail, and having with them, a few years ago, Little Tiger, Big Tiger, Old Tiger, Ellick, and Chipco, the last of whom was among the bravest fighters in the last Indian war.

The patient Parker sat on the sand hour after hour, imparting to us such information as we desired; and as we have never seen many Seminole words in print, we submit a portion of our vocabulary to our readers, merely remarking that if they do not wish to read the list, they can "skip it" and turn to something more to their mind.

INDIAN SCALP-DANCE.

The Seminole word for "a mile" is *akiska*; "How many miles?" is *akiska aachoma!*
"An axe" is *potsasna*; "an arm," *chesukpa*; "a boat," *pishloo*; "a book," *nscotsce'*; "beads," *kokose'*; "a bear," *nokose'*, and "a boy," *onunawah*.
"A camp" is *istalapo'*; "an Indian camp," *istachattahapo'*. "A crow" is *oshahawah*; "a cabbage-palmetto," *tallahako'*. When an article is cheap they say, *niskiheta'*.
"A deer" is *ichoo'*; "don't know" is *stuntosh*; "a deer-skin" is *ichoo-hablepe'*; "a dipper," *ahloo'*.
"To eat" is *humbuxjay*; "Me eat," *hompala'na*.
"Fire" is *totkah'*.
"Good" is *hitletutsjay*; "no good," *holowaukus*.
"Go" is *hiepusjay*; "Me go," *ahnetiepusjay*.
"A girl" is *nocktoche'*.
"Hungry" is *lotokowo*; "Me hungry," *salowetutsjay*.
"How many?" *nachoma!* "How much?" *innachomah!*
"House," *choko'*; "Indian house," *istachatta choko*.
"A huckleberry" is *chafakana*.
"A knife" in Seminole is *slafkah*; "a pocket-knife," *slafkah pootskah*.
"The moon" is *hutlisshe'*; "a moccasin," *stillepikah*.
"Me" (I), *ahne'*; "Me buy um," *nesalanesjay*; "money" (dollar), *shatokonowah*; "man," *hoonuntakah*.
"Pipe" is *chippakawah*; "potato," *ahkah*.
"A rabbit" is *chofe'*; "raccoon," *wootkoa*; "rifle," *itsah*; "breech-loading rifle," *itsasolotkah*; "road," *nene'*; "rain," *ooski*; "rock," *chato'*; "river," *weahlaka*.
"See-um," *hitsutlesjay*; "Me sleep," *notsepalanaste'*; "shoe," *stillepika onchay*; "smoke," *hoputka*; "smoke-skin," *chosseah*; "sand-hill crane," *watula'*; "squaw," *kooktakah*.
"Thunder" is *tenitskah'*.
"A wood-ibis" is *kakatawah*; probably so called from its cackling cries.
"A wolf" is *yaha'*; "to write," *hotsa'chen*. "What you call um?" *nagatoche'ftake'!*
"A woman" is *koktakah'*.
"Yes," *hungkah*; "you," *chime'*; "You go," *chimetiepusj*; "You got um?" *chemocha!*

The Seminole system of numeration is very complete, up to even a million.

"One" is *humkin*; 2, *hokolin*; 3, *totschnen*; 4, *orstan*; 5, *shako'bin*; 6, *epah'ken*; 7, *ko'lopahken*; 8, *ke'napahken*; 9, *orstapahken*; 10, *pahlen*; 11, *pahlen-humkin*; 12, *pahlen-hokolin*; etc.

It is supposed that the Seminoles, like many other wild Indians, used the fingers as aids in counting; hence we find their system one of fives and its multiples.

One of our number had with him an old book written more than a hundred years ago by a bluff old sailor named Romans, and it was interesting to compare that author's accounts with our own observations. In relation to the settlement of this continent he says: "I am firmly of the opinion that God created an original man and woman in this part of the globe, of different species from any in the other parts;" and then he goes on to show the difference between the white people and these savages native to America. "Our women," he says, "carry their children with their faces towards their own; a she savage puts the back of hers towards her own back. When we make a fire we pile the fuel parallel to each other; the savage puts his wood in a circular form, lights the central ends, and by the help of one of the sticks, which he shoves always to the centre, he keeps it alive. We make war in an open way; a savage, by hiding himself, surprises the enemy. Our prisoners are sure of life; those of the savage are sure to die by cruel tortures. When we take a sweat we keep ourselves warm, with the utmost care; a savage, with the pores of his skin open, plunges into an icy river or through a hole in the ice,"—and so forth.

After these generalizations, the old author speaks of the Creeks and Seminoles, ancestors of the present red men of Florida, whose customs are similar in every way. "I must relate," he says, "a particular custom of these people: when a deer or bear is killed by them they divide the liver into as many pieces as there are fires in camp, and send a boy to each with a piece, that the men belonging to each fire may burn it; but the fires of the women are excluded from this ceremony, and if each party kills one or more animals, the livers of each are treated in the same manner.

"Like all other savages, they are very fond of dogs, insomuch as never to kill one out of a litter. It is not an uncommon thing, in the nation, to see a dog so very lean that it has to seek a wall or post for its support before venturing to bark.

"They bury their dead in a square pit under the cabin, lining the grave with cypress-bark and placing the corpse in it in a sitting posture, as though alive, depositing with him his gun, tomahawk, pipe, and such other matters as he had the greatest regard for in his lifetime.

"In the Choctaw nation the dead are placed on an elevated stage till dried up, when a set of elderly gentlemen with very long finger-nails scrape the bones, deposit them in a chest, and paint the skull vermilion. At the end of a year the friends and relatives gather around, take the chest down from its shelf, weep over the bones, brighten up the color of the head, and then leave the

INDIAN BURIAL-PLACE.

remains to lasting oblivion. An enemy or a suicide was considered unworthy such attentions, and was at once buried and forgotten."

In regard to the great mounds of earth and shell which are found throughout Florida, this writer says: "This region was possessed by the Cherokees on the arrival of the Europeans, but they were afterwards dispossessed by the Creeks; though neither nation had any traditions for what purpose the mounds were built. Nor even had the nation they had previously dispossessed. All the country for many ages preceding the Cherokee invasion must have been inhabited by one tribe or nation, possessing one system of government, customs, and language.

"The language of these people is very agreeable to the ear; the women, in particular, speak in so musical a manner as to remind one of the singing of birds, and when heard and not seen one might imagine it to be the prattling of young children. The men's speech is, indeed, more strong and sonorous, but not harsh, and in no instance guttural.

"Seminole courtship in the olden time, as to day it is, was very simple. When a young man is determined to marry, and has fixed his affections, he takes a cane or reed, and repairs to the habitation of his beloved, attended by his friends and associates. In the presence of these wedding-guests, he sticks his reed upright in the ground; soon after, his sweetheart comes forth with another reed, which she sticks down by the side of his. This constitutes the ceremony of marriage; then they exchange reeds, which are laid by as certificates of the event, which is celebrated with feasting, music, and dancing, each one of their relatives contributing something to the new couple in their home."

It would seem to be an easy thing to get a divorce in this case, for one would only have to hide his stick or burn it, and then the other would have no proof visible of the ceremony.

More than an ordinary interest attaches to the forlorn remnant of this once powerful tribe, which, within the memory of the older portion of our people, held undisputed possession of the greater part of Florida. It is thought that Florida was once held by the fierce Caribs; later, the equally savage and untamable Yemassees overran the territory, when they, in turn, were dispossessed and finally exterminated by the Seminoles, or Lower Creeks. Whence came this powerful nation, or when they first occupied the territory held by them when first discovered by Europeans, is unknown. Traditions are insufficient to preserve historical facts. It is a notable circumstance that no tradition survives of De Soto's great march of two years among the Choctaws, Chicasaws, Cherokees, or Creeks, though he met and conquered thousands of red men, and left a trail of blood wherever he went.

> "From the memory of the old men
> Pass away the great traditions,
> The achievements of the warriors,
> The adventures of the hunters."

Their traditions state that, a long time ago, some wandering clans of Indians from the Northwest found their way to the present States of Alabama and Georgia. There, meeting with plenty of game, they settled in the vicinity of the then powerful tribes of the Florida and Appalachian Indians, who once overspread the country from the capes of Florida to the Mississippi. Gradually acquiring strength with their growth, the Seminoles successfully attacked and incorporated into their confederacy all the tribes within their reach, and became famous and prosperous. Extending themselves northward and eastward, as the supplies of game began to diminish, they settled along the principal rivers of Georgia and South Carolina. They subdued the Alabama nation, and won their good-will by restoring their river and territory. It was ever their policy to annex and make allies of powerful tribes, rather than weaken themselves in efforts of extermination. If the red men had pursued this policy in the early years of our Union, far different would have been their history.

The original Seminole nation soon divided, and became known by distinctive appellations. The northern Indians — by far the most numerous and wealthy — were known as the Creeks or Muscogees; they possessed a fertile and well-watered country, and consequently were able in war and successful in the field. The tribes or clans choosing the southern hunting-grounds retained the old title of Seminoles. Their country was poor and barren; and though numerous, they were obliged to separate into small bands in order to obtain subsistence. Well are they named. Peculiarly significant is their distinctive appellation of Seminole: *Ishti Semolli*, — "wild men, lost men." Wanderers upon the face of the earth have they been from the earliest record of their lives. In the latter part of the last century they inhabited the most fertile portions of northern and western Florida. Their principal town was Micasuka. They were styled the "Lower Creeks," in contradistinction to the Upper Creeks of Georgia and Carolina.

From the many different tribes that had been incorporated into the Creek confederacy, the original Seminole tongue was constantly undergoing changes and modulations. Only among the Lower Creeks or Seminoles was it spoken in its purity, and then only by a few of the oldest and most respectable of the women and chiefs, who made it a religious duty to instruct the young in the language of their ancestors, which, however, was soon forgotten and lost in the frequent use of the speech of the majority.

AN INCIDENT IN INDIAN WARFARE.

The Seminoles were constantly receiving additions to their number from the Upper Creeks who were driven south by the whites, from vagrants and outlaws of other tribes, and from escaped negroes and white men. Their country being a place of refuge for all, equally welcome were they made, in the simplicity of the Seminole heart. This accounts for the many broils and disturbances; for the Seminole was, essentially and peculiarly, a peace-loving and agricultural nation, from the first. They resided in log houses, cultivated crops of beans, potatoes, and corn, and lived a life of peace, so far as they were permitted.

Though several minor difficulties had occurred during the impetuous campaign of General Jackson, the disposition of the Seminole was pacific, and he committed no wanton or unprovoked attack. From the period of the cession of Florida to the United States, in 1821, there commenced a system of petty hostilities by the resident whites who desired the land, and by the settlers of Georgia who wanted the negroes of the Seminoles. Many negroes had fled for protection to the Seminole nation, and had been received as equals. The Indians also held slaves of their own; for the example of their white brother, in this respect, they were not slow to emulate. Though the white settlers, with truth, could claim many of the Seminole negroes, they also claimed and sought to obtain possession of many owned by the Indians, whom the latter had bought and paid for.

By various means and in many ways did the white man seek remuneration for the property his red brother held; but chiefly was this sought and obtained by means of treaties, by which the white man thought to induce the aborigines to emigrate to the far West. The treaty of Fort Moultrie in 1823 assigned the Indians a portion of territory, fixing the northern limits; and they were induced to give up their fields and villages for considerations which, they claimed, were never paid.

In 1832 such was the pressure brought to bear upon Congress and the executive of the State, that the Indians were assembled, represented by their principal chiefs, and induced to sign articles which were preliminary to a final agreement by them to leave the State and settle at the West. After an examination of the country by their chiefs, the majority of whom reported adversely, they were given two years to assemble for emigration. As the time drew near for their departure, the feeling of bitterness and hate that the preceding years had seen engendered by unscrupulous white men grew deeper, and they resolved that, sooner than leave their native land, they would fight the hated white man to the last. The war that ensued is a matter of history. It was begun by the massacre of Colonel Dade and his band of one hundred men, in December,

1835, and it was waged with unparalleled vindictiveness for seven years. It called into action such generals as Scott, Taylor, Gaines, Clinch, and Worth, and taxed the energies of many thousand men to subdue it. It developed new traits in the Indian character, showing that the peaceful agriculturist could be as relentless as the warrior who had trod the war-trail all his days. It showed what a feeble but desperate and determined people could do when aroused.

The Indian chiefs that assumed the control and direction of the Seminoles won the respect, if not the admiration, of their foes. The wily Osceola, the quick and generous Coacoochie, the treacherous Tusteauggee, and the desperate Philip have proved themselves worthy and respected foes.

At the conclusion of the war, in 1843, but a small remnant of the nation was left. Of the fifteen hundred warriors at the commencement of hostilities, but a paltry hundred or so remained in the State at its close. The remainder had either been killed, carried into captivity, or compelled to emigrate.

Since that outbreak the Indians have resided upon lands reserved for them in the southern part of the peninsula, hunting, and tilling their lands. One or two feeble outbreaks have given evidence that the old fire yet slumbers; but since 1858 there has been no serious difficulty with them.

There are at present between two hundred and three hundred Seminoles in Florida; but any accurate estimate of their number is prevented by their vigilance in keeping themselves concealed in the swamps and fastnesses of the interior and the regions of the Everglades. The number of families, as related by the most intelligent chiefs, is about fifty. Upon the borders of Lake Okechobee is the largest settlement, of thirty families. In the gloomy swamps of the Big Cypress, southwest of Lake Okechobee, are from five to eight more, of the most sullen and unconquerable, who shun all intercourse with white men. In the Everglades, some ten miles from the shore of Biscayne Bay, upon the Atlantic coast, are from ten to fifteen families. Upon Pease Creek, a stream flowing into the Gulf of Mexico, are some seven or eight families.

To resolve the different settlements into their radical lineage and go back to the period when tribes of different blood roamed over the State, it would be correct to say that the Okechobee Indians are Seminoles, pure and simple; the Everglade Indians, the Micasukees, are a peculiar offshoot of the Creeks; and the gloomy inhabitants of the Big Cypress are Creeks who were forced (or, rather, whose ancestors were) to join in the war, having been driven from Georgia in the fierce and bloody wars that ensued prior to the Seminole War in Florida.

These Indians hold little intercourse with the whites; occasional trading-visits to the coast being the limit of their communication with them, when they exchange dressed deer-skins, sil... ornaments, and sweet-potatoes for the

DEATH OF KING PHILIP.

necessaries of life that the trader keeps in stock, — calico, ammunition, beads, and the much loved whiskey. For the last, though not so immoderate as their Western relatives, they will go any lengths, and do anything to obtain it. The Seminole makes a business of intoxication, and devotes himself exclusively to getting drunk, when the mood and state of his finances will allow. He carries to the trading-post his stock of deer and bear skins, wild honey, beeswax; his wife takes her agricultural products — sweet-potatoes, generally; and after purchasing and begging all the articles deemed necessary to their support and adornment, they invest the rest in whiskey. So methodical are they in this matter that they have sometimes left the trading-post without buying the whiskey, not willing to deprive themselves or their families of the more necessary articles. But, the whiskey being purchased, they proceed to enjoy it. They first — generally this is done — place their knives and rifles in a place of safety in charge of the women, when they give themselves up to the free and unrestrained enjoyment of their dearly bought pleasure. They get very "high," boisterous, tipsy, "tight." In their drunken fits they perform all sorts of extravagances. Sober-looking, dignified chiefs, their heads whitened by the burdens of seventy years, will dance and shout with the agility and hilarity of youth. Their drunken sprees generally end without bloodshed, even without a quarrel, and they expend their energies in shouting and whooping themselves hoarse. The women wait patiently until their lords have recovered their senses, and then they are allowed to inebriate a little on their own account.

Bartram, a writer and botanist who visited the Seminoles over a century since, gives an amusing description of one of their drunken frolics, and tells how the women then procured their share of the liquor. He says: "The men go about in a joyful state, and whenever they meet a woman, insist upon her drinking. This she pretends to do; but, after taking a good mouthful of the whiskey, she discharges it into a bottle concealed in her mantle. This is repeated until sometimes the bottle is filled; and she afterward, when the drunken wretches have wasted their liquor, sells it to the braves at her own price."

In many things the Seminole is superior to his white brother. His uniform gentleness and courtesy to his family are noteworthy. In his trading-expeditions his wife and children always receive their share of purchases, and some little trinket or article of apparel is always bought for the latter. They are ignorant, yet enlightened; neglectful of many interests which the white man considers essential to happiness and prosperity, yet attentive to many considerations of which the white man would do well to be mindful.

They adopt the dress and habits of the whites, so far as they do not interfere with their wild instincts of the chase. Their cabins are of logs, but open at both ends. They wear the homespun shirt of the white man, but the leggings and moccasins of their forefathers. They cannot read or write, yet they have a complete numerical system which answers every purpose.

If we accept the statement of Washington Irving, there is a deep-seated reason for the Seminole ignorance of reading and writing. This is the graceful writer's Seminole tradition: —

"We have a tradition handed down from our forefathers, and we believe it, that the Great Spirit, when he undertook to make men, made the black man. It was his first attempt, and pretty well for a beginning; but he soon saw that he had bungled, so he determined to try his hand again. He did so, and made the red man. He liked him much better than the black man, but still he was not exactly what he wanted. So he tried once more, and made the white man, and then he was satisfied. You see, therefore, that you were made last, and that is the reason I call you my youngest brother.

"When the Great Spirit had made the three men, he called them together and showed them three boxes. The first was filled with books and maps and papers; the second with bows and arrows, knives and tomahawks; the third with spades, axes, hoes, and hammers. 'These, my sons,' said he, 'are the means by which you are to live; choose among them according to your fancy.'

"The white man, being the favorite, had the first choice. He passed by the box of working tools without notice; but when he came to the weapons for war and hunting, he stopped and looked hard at them. The red man trembled, for he had set his heart upon that box. The white man, however, after looking upon it for a moment, passed on, and chose the box of books and papers. The red man's turn came next, and you may be sure he seized with joy upon the bows and arrows and tomahawks. As to the black man, he had no choice left but to put up with the box of tools.

"From this, it is clear that the Great Spirit intended the white man should learn to read and write, to understand all about the moon and stars, and to make everything, even rum and whiskey; that the red man should be a first-rate hunter, and a mighty warrior, but he was not to learn anything from books, as the Great Spirit had not given him any; nor was he to make rum and whiskey, lest he should kill himself with drinking. As to the black man, as he had nothing but working tools, it was clear he was to work for the white and red man, which he has continued to do. We must go according to the wishes of the Great Spirit, or we shall get into trouble. To know how to read and write is very good for white men, but very bad for red men. It makes white men better, but red men worse."

BURIAL OF DE SOTO.

CHAPTER XIII.

SOMETHING ABOUT CAMPING OUT.

FLORIDA abounds in wonders, with its underground lakes and rivers, its curious birds, beasts, and fishes; and many of its possessions may be seen in a journey along its largest river, the St. John's. Flowing through swamp and forest and prairie, it brings down with it, from the almost unknown source of its existence, a suggestion of mysterious regions as yet unpenetrated. Though the broad surface of its lower waters is crossed by many a craft of sportsman-tourist, yet none has penetrated beyond a certain little lake, surrounded by marshes of reeds and canes.

Lake Washington, more than three hundred miles from the mouth of the St. John's, is the last navigable water, and few have ever reached it. On its eastern shore a fringe of low willows borders a rolling swell of upland, upon which are growing a few wind-torn palmettos, wild oranges, and persimmons. This little isolated mound shows traces of cultivation in some time long past; and an occasional shard of pottery, or arrow-head of flint or shell, gives color to the tradition that this was an Indian field, cultivated by the red man many years before the advent of the white man.

Beneath the rustling leaves of the palmettos, basking in the sunshine of a March afternoon, two young men lay watching a wreath of smoke which, proceeding from some source unseen, was floating over the prairie, dancing here and there, north, east, and west, in a manner most unaccountable. This smoke-wreath came from the stack of a diminutive steamer, the "Starlight," which had laboriously steamed all the way from the civilized portion of the lower St. John's to bring these young men to this, the farthest limit of navigation.

It was the first time in years the trip had been taken, and the adventures of that voyage would have made a lasting impression upon the voyagers, had they not already been eclipsed by their earlier explorations. For these two (it is perhaps needless to explain) were no other than the Antiquarian and the Historian, who, finding they could not reach the head-waters of the St. John's with all their "plunder" by an overland journey, had taken sailing-craft to the mouth of the great river, and thence, by the way of Jacksonville, had chartered the little steamer to bring them back to this place, within less than one hundred miles of their starting-point.

We will not discuss the wisdom of this undertaking; but they were after adventure, and they took this method of finding it.

The letters they had sent back by that little steamer — their last connection with civilization for several weeks — were replete with the experiences of their sail up that mighty river. The night passed in a narrow channel, fast in a mud-bank, surrounded by clouds of mosquitoes, when the booming and clanging clamor of thousands of water-fowl filled their ears and prevented sleep; the days of monotonous steaming against the sluggish current, cautiously threading narrow channels through the dense canebrakes, where the canes met above the deck; the deer they saw, and the turkeys they shot. — all these were fully described in their letters. From one of the Historian's we take this account of their trip: —

> The steamer was a curiously contrived affair, its motive power in the stern, in the shape of a paddle-wheel; and everything, even to the smoke-stack, was

A CURIOUS FLOATING ISLAND

"housed," to prevent being swept away by overhanging trees. The berths were narrow, and the room limited; but during the day we stayed on deck, with rifles ready for deer and alligators, or sat astern, above the foaming water of the paddle-wheel, and trolled for bass.

On the lower river long stretches of gray cypress, miles in extent, were relieved by dark green clumps of magnolias and live-oaks, while a few cleared places indicated plantations and orange-groves.

After crossing famous Lake George, we entered a narrower channel, where the palms grew close to the water's edge, and the banks narrowed upon the river until the hanging festoons of Spanish moss nearly swept the steamer's deck. Floating islands of water-lettuce, rods in breadth, spangled with flowers and alive with water-birds, were set adrift by the waves and floated idly down the stream with their living freight. At times we passed the mouths of creeks, where the clearer water was alive with fish, — pike, perch, and bass, — and were supplied by springs, which boiled up from great depths.

At Lake Harney was passed the site of old King Philip's town, an Indian village once in possession of a noted Seminole chief; and at intervals loomed up mounds of earth raised by the Indians ages ago, to commemorate some great chief or important epoch of Indian life. So many creeks and bayous opened out of the river, that any less experienced man than Captain Jones, of the "Starlight," would have been perplexed to keep the channel; especially when nearing Lake Washington, which was approached through a series of vast marshy plains. We reached the lake in the forenoon, unloaded the steamer, sent back our message to friends at home, and the afternoon found us preparing to camp.

As the shades of evening drew near we bestirred ourselves in getting up the camp. We had with us our small boat, and this was heavily laden with provisions for two months' time, just as it had been landed from the steamer in the hurry of departure. A half-barrel of flour, securely hooped, lay on the sand; near it a keg of pork, a barrel of hard-tack and one of potatoes, and a box containing smaller articles necessary for subsistence, such as salt, pepper, mustard, condensed milk, raw coffee, a little tea, sugar, and a few pickles. One little keg, securely bound with iron hoops, contained two gallons of whiskey, which, as neither of us used the "ardent," seemed superfluous. But let the following letter explain its being found in our possession. It was written by Jim Scobie, whom we left on Mosquito Lagoon, and who had promised to join us here and take us to the haunts of heron and turkey.

NEW SMYRNA, FLA., March 9, 18—.

DEER SIRS,— If you will be at Lake Washington in just one month from too da, at the injun feild on the east side of the lake, I will be there O. K.

Git Capn Jones to take you on the starlite, he and me went up there once and he knos the channel like a book, and better for he can't rede.

Fit out with what I told you and take a good stock of tobacko and a little wisky for the stomuks sake you kno. Don't forgit the wisky, for the stomuks sake, as you might be bit by snaiks which it is the only remedy for snaik-bites.

Aligaters is plenty where I'm going to take you, and dere and turkeys just heeps of em and we can make a heep of money on their hides.

All other directions I told yu last time I saw yu. Send the wisky along sure, as they don't have any here worth drinking — for snaik-bites, I mean ; better send enuff.

Yures till deth,

JAMES SCOBIE.

The whiskey, then, was brought along for "snake-bites" that Jim might be troubled with, though for ourselves we had little apprehension.

One of our boxes held a small quantity of arsenic, alcohol, carbolic acid, and such like for preservatives for use in case we met with any rare and curious animals.

An old trunk, half full of clothes, held also two rubber ponchos, with buttoned slits in the centre, from which water-proof cloaks could be quickly fashioned when it rained, some heavy woollen blankets, and strips of mosquito-netting made into "bars," for protection from the inevitable insect. A keg of powder, several bags of shot, and boxes of ammunition, with a rifle, revolver, and shot-gun each, completed our armament.

Unfastening the line that wrapped the roll of blankets, I withdrew a canvas, carried it up beneath the palmettos, and there spread it upon the ground, disclosing a small tent I had made on the voyage.

Taking an axe, the Antiquarian went off in search of poles for the support of the tent, and for some soft substance for bedding. He was successful in finding the bedding, hanging from some broad-limbed oaks in the shape of long skeins and festoons of the gray *tillandsia*, or "Spanish moss." Climbing the trees, he threw down a large heap, and then carried it to the spot selected for the camp and spread it out a foot deep; over this a layer of palmetto-fans, then the rubber ponchos, and then the blankets. Thus the bed was made; and it looked sufficiently inviting, although not of softest down, to be occupied at once.

But he could n't find anywhere a tree small enough for the tent-poles. "I never saw such a country in all my life," he growled to me. "Just

AN UNPLEASANT NEIGHBOR.

look at these pines; nothing but pine-trees for miles and miles; not a bush or shrub beneath them, and not a branch or limb on their trunks for forty feet. Here I've been hunting an hour or more, and can't find a branch, even, large enough or small enough for a ridge-pole. The fires have burned all the fallen limbs, and the branches of the few oaks are too scraggy and crooked."

"Well," I answered, "perhaps we sha'n't need a tent to-night; we must get accustomed to sleeping without one. But why can't we make the oars and the sprit of the sail answer for supports?"

"So we can; I did n't think of that. Bear a hand, now, and the house goes up to-night."

It was n't long before the sprit was made fast at one end to the trunk of a tree, the other supported upon the crossed blades of the oars lashed together, the canvas thrown over them, and the tent-pins driven into the sand. A fire was then kindled at the foot of an old stump; and in the frying-pan, supported upon a pile of bones, the pork was soon sizzling briskly.

"Bring up some of those sweet-potatoes that we bought of the Cracker at Lake Harney, and a handful of hard-tack," commanded the Antiquarian; "brown some of the coffee in the skillet, pound it in a shot-bag, and we'll soon have supper ready, and sooner disposed of, I'm thinking. Now, 'take a cher,' as these Florida Crackers say, and 'dror up' to the table."

"Speaking of Crackers," said I, "do you remember that specimen we met at Fort Pierce, the one who volunteered to collect beetles for the Doctor? He came into camp, while you were away, with five or six palm-beetles, which he had dug out of a rotten palmetto.

"'Doc.,' he drawled, 'I've got some curosties fer yer; yis, sir, I hev, an' thet's a fack.'

"'Well, I'll take them,' said the Doctor, 'and thank you kindly.'

"'Yis, Doc., but we-uns can't live on thankee-kindly; we-uns has to hev hog an' homony. I reck'n I've got to charge ye somef'n fer them there critters, Doc.; they'se guv me a heap uv trouble, an' I grubbed fur 'em right-smart, I did, Doc., bet yer boot-jack!'

"'All right! How much do you want for them?'

"The beetles were worthless; but the Doctor always made a point of taking everything the natives brought him, because he sometimes got valuable finds.

"'Waal,' drawled the Cracker, 'them's val'ble critters, them is; but I reck'n you-uns can hev 'em at about tew dollars apiece.'

"'Two dollars apiece?' demanded the astonished naturalist.

"'Thet's what I said, Doc.'

"'But, my dear friend, don't you think they're worth more than that?'

ONE OF THE DOCTOR'S FINDS.

"The Cracker scratched his head, and looked, if possible, more foolish than usual. 'Yis, I s'pose they 'se wuth moh, an' I ought tew ask moh; but I 'lowed we-uns did n't know *how much yew Yankees could stand!*'"

"Yes, that's it," mused the Antiquarian; "that's the key-note of their tune down here, — how much we Yankees will endure. It is said, you know, that they themselves admit that they live on 'taters an' pone in the summer, and on the Yankees in the winter.' But I think this Jim Scobie we have engaged to meet us will treat us well; at all events, I wish he were here, and shall hope to see him by to-morrow."

The conversation languished as darkness fell, and soon after the stars came out we sought our blankets beneath the canvas; the fire sputtered fitfully awhile, and then went out, and no noises broke the stillness of this solitary spot, save the hootings of the owls and the mournful cries of the chuck-wills-widows.

CHAPTER XIV.

A TURKEY-HUNT IN THE PINY WOODS.

T dawn, next morning, I felt a chill presentiment of a disagreeable arrival in camp, as I lay half asleep. Rousing myself with an effort, I opened my eyes and looked straight up into the face of a man who was bending over me. I had hardly time to cry out, when the man seized my hand, and shook it cordially; for it was no other than Jim Scobie, who had come across from Indian River on foot.

"Yis, sir, I waited till arter moon-up, an' then streaked it acrost to you-uns. Well, how are you-uns, anyhow? I'm right smart peart, myself, and hopes you-uns am the same. Now, if you-uns don't object, I'll jest take charge uv this camp, and set yer up right all ready to go out huntin' soon as sun-up."

The proprietors did n't object; and Jim, leaning his long rifle against a tree and hanging on it his game-pouch, set about making a fire, the cheery flame of which was very comforting in the damp of the morning; so the inmates of the tent crawled out half dressed, and completed their toilet by the fire.

Jim moved about as though completely familiar with the surroundings, found without trouble the provisions, and soon had the omnipresent pork frying in the pan, and a pot of coffee boiling beside it.

In the midst of his labors his attention was arrested by the little iron-hooped keg, for which he immediately conceived a warm interest; he eyed it intently, then took it up and "hefted" it, set it down carefully, and finally put it up to his nose and took a good whiff at the bung.

"Thet's the stuff, dog-gone me ef 't ain't,—the reg'lar snake-medicine, boys, an' it was rale thoughtful uv yer to brung it. Dog-my-cats ef I ain't afeard I shall be snake-bit to-day ef I don't hist in some of thet ther snake-juice plum-quick. Here's to ye, boys; may yer never be snake-bit!"

It was rather "airly in the day," as Jim explained, to begin "a-histin'" in liquor; but there had been a whiskey famine on Indian River for nearly a month, and he couldn't resist the opportunity to indulge.

His hosts, though willing to indulge any respectable whim of this vagrant hunter, were not going to allow him unstinted use of the liquor, and this they told him; but Jim protested that he had no intention of using it to excess, and that, as all he wanted was one heavy dram, they might lock it up for the rest of the day.

Then he returned to his frying-pan; and as he got warmed up (either through the internal or external heat applied) he became communicative, unfolding a plan for the day's sport.

"As I kem along, boys, by the ten-mile slew, I see somef'n thet made me ache to stop; but I thought how much you-uns might like to be thar tew, an' so I kep' on,— I kep' on. What was it I see? Well, I didn't *see* nuffin'; but I *heerd*,— yis, boys, I *heerd*. What did I heerd? Well, boys, dog-gone my buttons ef I didn't heerd the all-firedest gobblin' in the hammock thet ever I heerd in all my borned days."

"Turkeys!" shouted the Antiquarian and I in one breath.

"Turkeys!" calmly replied Jim; "and a whole fambly uv 'em, at that."

"Well, then, let's go after them now."

"Thet's what I wus goin' to remark when you-uns busted in onto me so suddint-like. Jest es soon's you-uns hes eat them hog an' taters, we'll light out arter the gobblers."

To dispose of breakfast was now a short proceeding, and in less than twenty minutes "we-uns" were entirely equipped for a turkey-hunt. Jim whistled up his cur-dog, Satan, and after feeding him on the scraps left over from breakfast, took up his gun and strode out of camp, followed by his eager employers. And while we are on the trail to the turkey-roost, let us glance at the wild turkey in his native home.

Time was when this "most delicious, as it is the largest and noblest, of all gallinaceous game" might have been taken in almost any State east of the Rocky Mountains; but now the would-be wild-turkey hunter must seek his game in the southern and western portions of our Union. In the Southern States, especially Florida, any one, even the veriest pot-hunter, may secure his bird, provided he has money enough. The sudden appearance of a flock of wild turkeys upon the banks of the upper St. John's, as the steamer rounds some wooded point, is not of uncommon occurrence.

Their relative abundance in any particular locality depends upon the supply of their favorite mast,— nuts, acorns, etc., and the seed of the palmetto,

THE HOME OF THE HERON.

wherever found. Their presence is indicated to the experienced hunter by their
"scratching-places;" and he can tell by the freshness of them, and the character
of the surrounding forest, where to look for them. In October the males have
in a great measure recovered their strength and plumpness, the females their
good condition, and the young are able to take care of themselves, and withal
are tender and juicy. Then, according to Audubon, the males and females
hunt in separate parties. At this time the gobblers may be enticed within shot
by the hunter lying concealed and imitating the clucking sound of the hen.
Of the various methods employed, probably this is the most successful, though
even this may be better used in spring. Old hunters are adepts in the art of
calling, and their peculiar inimitable call is something the gobbler is hardly
proof against, provided the hunter lies close. Sometimes, however, he will
answer the call without putting in an appearance, thus depriving the worthy
hunter of his meal. The best call, by the way, is made from the wing-bone of
the turkey itself, though tolerably good ones may be obtained from dealers in
sporting goods.

The old style of trapping the bird in pens is, of course, out of the question,
except to residents in a good turkey country.

Shooting by moonlight, also, is only to be indulged in by the occupants
of turkey-haunted sections, though those favored beings whose lives are cast
in such places may depopulate an entire neighborhood in a short time.

Probably the most sportsmanlike method of procedure would be to hunt
with dogs, though even then the sport savors of pot-hunting, as it is rarely a
wing-shot can be procured, for the turkey soon takes to tree, and must be
sought out, like the ruffed grouse when in similar position. Like the grouse,
too, it remains perfectly immovable, and is often overlooked.

It is in early spring, and early in the morning, when the gobblers are
saluting each other from the different tree-tops, that a good hunter may expect
sport. Then his success depends upon his skill in threading the tangled
thicket without noise, and in nearing the wary bird unperceived. If he wishes
to bring that bird to bay, he must move with the rapidity of a deer when
necessary, and at times stand motionless as a stump; for there is no more
suspicious bird than an old gobbler who knows that he is informing a whole
forest of his presence. It may be unsportsmanlike; it may be pot-hunting;
but there is a deal of satisfaction in seeing a plump fifteen-pounder drop from
his airy perch at the report of your gun, especially when you need his presence in camp. Frank Forester says that though he is always delighted to
see a well-roasted turkey on the board, especially if well stuffed with truffles
and served up with well-dressed bread-sauce, he wouldn't give the least pala-

table mouthful of him — no, not his undevilled gizzard — to pot-hunt a thousand in such a style. But then, he never shot one. The weight of the hen turkey, full grown, should be about ten pounds; gobblers, from fifteen to twenty, though instances are related of the capture of thirty-five pounders. Though a full-grown bird will carry away a heavy load in the body, a charge of an ounce and a half of number two shot, backed by three drachms of good powder, well placed in the neck or head, will always prove effective. Even number eight shot have proved too much for young males, though hunters generally prefer buck-shot.

The Florida hunters "call" wild turkeys from October to April. The birds begin to mate about the last of February and the first of March. They can only be called when they are scattered; then go in the direction they take, and sit down and call the old hens when the young are about, by imitating their whistle somewhat mixed up with their gobbles.

The best time to hunt them is in the winter, when the leaves are dry and the turkeys are scratching, as they then make so much noise as to be heard a long way, and give the hunter time to slip in upon them unperceived.

It was about an "hour by sun" when we started for the turkey-grounds. At first our route lay through the pine-woods, after leaving which we entered a marsh with the mud up to our knees. Wading through the marsh, the next feature of the journey was a cypress-swamp; and of all the dismal, even repulsive places, this was the worst. There were broad, stagnant pools, black as ink, with old stumps and dead branches scattered through them, and in the foul mud we would sink knee-deep.

We waded through this dismal swamp for nearly an hour, seeing no living thing other than ourselves; and it was with a heartfelt sigh of relief that we emerged from its darkness and stood on firm ground beneath tall pines, looked through the long vistas between their tall trunks, and breathed the pure air laden with resinous odors.

The ground was covered with low scrub-palmetto, about two feet high, except at intervals, where occur spaces of sand with nothing growing but wire-grass.

It was a scene of solitude without dreariness. In a tall pine isolated from the rest was a great bulk of sticks, which a nearer examination revealed to be an eagle's nest, and going yet nearer we saw a beautiful bald eagle sailing high in the air overhead. This was a male eagle, with pure white head and neck; soon the female came flying over the tree-tops, and a well-directed shot from the Antiquarian's double-barrel brought her screaming to the ground. Throwing herself on her back, she extended her claws and awaited our coming, her eyes flashing defiance, her crooked beak gnashing savagely, and her crest bristling. The dog rushed in and seized her, though he received many severe gashes from the cruel claws, and only overcame her after a long and obstinate fight.

In the strip of woods beyond we saw our first wild turkey, running rapidly at first, and then taking to flight. This warned us to be cautious; and we did n't need Jim's warnings to cause us to tread softly, and make no noise whatever. It was a rather open bit of woods, between the swamp and the pine-barrens, where pines and palmettos grew in clusters, and the ground was covered with dead grass.

It was quite hot by this time, and we reclined awhile beneath a palmetto, while a slight breeze rustled the great palm-leaves and the pine-leaves quivered; but all else was quiet and dream-like.

Many warblers were twittering in the pines; graceful swallows performed aerial evolutions over the savannas; a red-shouldered hawk sent forth frequently its sharp cry; a little plover mourned in the copse, and high overhead three white-headed eagles were describing a series of circles in the pure atmosphere.

It seemed too quiet (as Jim remarked) for any game to be moving; and as it was late, no turkeys were gobbling, as they only gobble in early morning. So we had about concluded that our journey was destined to be barren of results, and that after a rest we would turn about for camp, when old Satan, in his goings to and fro in the scrub, suddenly gave out a short yelp, which brought us all to our feet in an instant.

Then, about a hundred yards away, up flew a wild turkey, followed by another and another, until three were in the air at once. As they were a little beyond the range of our guns, we were obliged to let them fly off unmolested; but as they had not seen us, and had only noticed the dog, they did not fly far, but alighted, one after the other, in some tall trees in a neighboring hammock.

"Now, boys," said Jim, "lay low and try to creep onto 'em in the hammock yander. You two spread a little apart, an' I'll take a line for that t' other hammock beyont, in case they sees you-uns and flies. Be keerful, now, for them ther animiles hes eyes es sharp es needles."

Satan, when he observed the direction taken by the turkeys, dashed off through the scrub in hot pursuit, although he must have known that it was out of the question to catch them; but his manœuvres served a good purpose, in diverting the attention of the birds, and enabling us to creep to within a long gunshot unobserved.

Selecting the largest turkey in sight, the Antiquarian "drew a bead" on it; and as the report of his gun broke the stillness, the others broke from their covert in precipitous flight.

I was not quite within range at this moment; but the two turkeys in the air chanced to fly right over my head, and by a fortunate wing-shot I brought down the foremost crashing through the trees.

Nor was this all; for the remaining bird, confused by the noise and smoke, wheeled around to the left, and passed directly over the Antiquarian, who was trying to note the exact spot in which his first game had fallen. His attention being attracted by the whirring of wings overhead, he was quick to avail himself of his opportunity, and with a sudden motion threw up his gun and stopped the flight of the noble bird right in mid-air.

A cheer from me announced that this extraordinary shot had a witness, and each of us darted forward to secure his fluttering prey.

Jim Scobie, who had traversed but half the distance to his destination, was puzzled to account for those three shots in rapid succession, but he wisely concluded that they meant three dead turkeys, in which case there were none left for him; so he changed his course and joined us at the hammock. And he was surprised!

"Dog-gone my picter!" he ejaculated, rubbing his chin with his horny palm, "ef I hed thunk you-uns would cleaned out the hull flock, you-uns would n't hev come along with we-uns."

But he was not half so vexed as he would have us believe, and at once helped us to find the turkey in the tree; after which we all paused to admire them. They were beautiful birds, good representatives of the *Meleagris gallopavo*, though not so large as some we had shot previously. They weighed, perhaps, a dozen pounds apiece; though we certainly thought that *thirty* was nearer the mark, after we had "toted" them into camp.

Shouldering a turkey each, we marched triumphantly back to the lake, tired and hungry when we arrived, and prepared to do justice to the "hog and taters" that Jim cooked over the light-wood fire as soon as possible after reaching our destination.

HERONS AND ALLIGATORS.

CHAPTER XV.

HERONS AND ALLIGATORS.

WE stayed in the vicinity of Lake Washington for nearly a week, thoroughly exploring the region, and then packed our belongings into the boat and descended southward to the body of water known as Salt Lake.

The surroundings of Salt Lake are of that unutterably dreary character which oppresses one like a nightmare; on every side stretched miles and miles of marsh and creek; nothing that indicated land could be seen except a circling line of trees dim in the distance.

But we had not come to Salt Lake in search of beautiful scenery; our object was to find good alligator-hunting and to add to our stock of information regarding the water-birds of Florida, especially the herons.

We pitched our tent in the pine-woods, about a mile from the landing, where there was everything needful except good water. It seemed a veritable paradise for marsh and water fowl; for the lake margin was covered with snipe and shore birds and the marshes were full of heron, while the lake itself was alive with trout or black bass, and dotted with the black forms of numerous alligators.

The instinct of the naturalist became rampant at sight of so much good game; and as soon as camp was fairly set in order we instituted a systematic search for the most desirable varieties of fish and fowl.

The second afternoon found us starting out on a heron-hunt: Jim Scobie being familiar with all this region and desirous to lead us out to a heron-roost which he declared to be the biggest in all eastern Florida.

Rowing across to the north side of the lake, we entered a creek which led us into the marsh, beyond which was a pond, and which we reached after hard rowing, poling, and wading through the half-submerged canes. The heronry, on the farther shore of the pond, was reached about sunset; and as we pulled towards it clouds of white herons flew up silently and made their way to the opposite shore.

Jim landed us on the muddy shore of the island, and then went off trolling for bass. The trees above us, and for a long distance around were covered with great nests of sticks, many of them over two feet in diameter, but so carelessly constructed that we could look through them all, and at times see the eggs that a few of them contained. Looking back upon that heron hunt, I can say that it was a shameful thing to do, — to shoot unsuspecting birds as they came winging their way joyfully home to their nests. It was a most inexcusable act; yet we did it, in the thoughtlessness of our search for the rare and curious, not giving heed then to the chidings of conscience — until we had shot the birds.

Since that time many a bird-collector has visited Florida, and the heronries and even the woods and fields have been terribly ravaged. I know of one worthless dealer in bird-skins who has in his collection hundreds of mockingbirds and cardinals, which he and his emissaries have killed. The most contemptible of these so-called naturalists are those who kill birds for the "hat trade," encouraged thereto by the prevalent fashion among females of wearing the skins of bright-colored birds in their hats. For the supplying of this demand, also, of feathers for the fair sex, the miserable collectors have visited and ravaged the heronries, shooting the birds and stripping off the beautiful plumes.

As the sun sank down behind the pines, scattered groups of herons came flying towards the island where we were concealed, — now a great white heron, now a small blue one, and occasionally a night heron.

The sun disappeared; the moon came out and shed a faint light over the marshes and the lonely island, disclosing to the watchers there the hurrying dusky forms in the sky, many of which fell at the fire of the marauders stationed beneath the trees.

It is a singular fact that a heron will take no notice of a still object, approaching it without suspicion and alighting close by, even if that object be a man; so we had many opportunities for observing the shape and action of the birds at close quarters.

When we left (I now grieve to state) we had nearly a score of herons of various kinds. Jim had caught a number of noble black bass, by trolling in the lake, and had thus provided for the morrow's breakfast. We again made our way over the marshes, almost waist-deep in water, until the creek was gained, when an hour's pull brought us to the landing-place. Gleaming white in the moonlight, our back-loads of herons appeared more like sheeted ghosts; and verily, if all wicked deeds are requited in kind, the slayers of those innocent birds deserved to have their nights disturbed during the remainder of their lives by the apparitions of their victims.

The excuse urged by the hunters is that they are working " in the interests of science;" but that is too flimsy a pretext for this intelligent age, and I sincerely trust that all those who do likewise will be unceremoniously bundled into jail, in the interest of humanity!

GREEN HERON.

During our camp near Salt Lake we found nearly every variety of heron native to Florida; and perhaps it would interest our readers to note the list of species mentioned below, according to their size: —

The Great White Heron (*Ardea occidentalis*) is a resident in the southern part of the State. The Great Blue Heron (*Ardea herodias*) is found everywhere; as are also the White Heron (*Ardea alba*) and the Snowy Heron (*Ardea candidissima*). This latter is one of the most beautiful and graceful of the family, with its dainty form, its delicate curling plumes, and garb of purest white.

A rarer bird is the Purple Heron (*Ardea rufescens*); while a very common variety is the Night Heron (*Ardea nycticorax*), also found throughout the Northern States. The Yellow-crowned Night Heron (*A. violacea*) is harder to find, seeking the depths of dismal swamps.

The Little Blue (*A. carulea*) and the Louisiana (*A. ludoviciana*) are as graceful of form and dainty-stepping as the Snowy; while the Green Heron is seen everywhere along the rivers and swamp-margins.

To complete the list, the Bittern (*Botaurus minor*) should be mentioned, and the smallest of all, the *Ardetta exilis*; the former found here every winter, and the latter all the time.

If we were to try to present a complete list of all the water-birds we found, it would convert the remainder of this volume into a mere catalogue; but we must not omit the Great Ibis (*Tantalus loculator*), nor the White Ibis (*Ibis alba*) both of them recalling to mind pictures of the sacred ibis of Egypt. The Scarlet Ibis, which more nearly resembles the Egyptian, is not now found in Florida, though in Audubon's time, some fifty years ago, it was said to come to the Keys in flocks.

Most curious of all Florida's water-birds is the so-called Snake-bird (*Plotus anhinga*), which may be seen on the St. John's, and which very much resembles a snake when swimming in the water.

It was at Salt Lake that we finally broke camp, paid Jim Scobie his wages and sent him home, and brought our tent and boat life to an end by paddling northward to the St. John's. A chain of lakelets connects Salt Lake with Snake Creek, through the crooked channel of which the great river is reached.

Before our departure, however, we had a last adventure with some alligators, that may perhaps be worthy of mention. Each of us wished for a pair of alligator boots, and at various times had shot and skinned a "'gator;" but the great reptiles were so numerous at Salt Lake that we could not forego an endeavor to add to our trophies.

One clear morning, just after sunrise, I poled away from the landing in our skiff, and skirted the southern shore, with an eye open for saurians. The glossy-backed grackles and fish-crows were cawing and cackling on the beach, and hundreds of heron were wading the still waters of the shallow lagoons.

My companions had gone out hunting for deer, and I was tempted to follow them; but hearing a distant shot, I concluded that they had found their game, and so, as it was too late, I kept on my way. I found out later that they had shot at a coon, and that while they were at breakfast the dog had started the deer, running them directly in front of the camp, the Antiquarian coming out just in time to see an antlered buck and a doe run by him within easy shot.

I saw an alligator, apparently asleep on a sand-bar and, rowing up within thirty or forty yards, placed a charge of duck-shot through his most vulnerable spot, just behind the eye. This stretched him out, to all appearances lifeless; and I left him there, clawing the sand spasmodically, while I moved farther down the shore looking for another.

This 'gator would measure all of nine feet, and his hide was large enough to furnish leather for several pairs of boots; but, unfortunately, not all the hide is available for boots. It takes a pair of alligators for each pair of boots; owing to the extreme thickness of the skin and its horniness, only the under portion is good for the purpose, and that, too, for but a limited distance from the under jaw, running backward towards the middle of the body. The best boots are made by taking the skin of the throat for the toe and "vamp," and that portion on the under side of the forelegs for the quarters and heel. By using the skins of a pair of alligators, the boots can be made to match each other in the size and shape of the scale-plates; the smallest and most flexible at the toes and running up larger and larger to the top. Boots made in this way from skins properly tanned, are very handsome and extremely durable; those I had made from the alligators shot that day lasted me longer than any others I ever possessed. But I anticipate, by this *post-mortem* statement, the shooting of the other 'gator.

I had proceeded but a quarter of a mile or so, and had rowed half-way round the lake, when I saw a black object floating on the water a little distance ahead. It resembled a gnarled pine-knot, worn by the water and blackened by the sun; but I knew it in an instant for an alligator. Judging by the length of its head, which was the part thus exposed, I concluded it to be a very large one, not less than ten feet in length.

Propelling the skiff a little nearer, I could see its evil-looking eye gleam sullenly, and a slight ripple behind it warned me that it was about to sink itself beneath the surface. At this I threw up my gun and sent a heavy charge of buck-shot directly into that glassy eye. Contrary to my expectations, the 'gator, instead of sinking or floundering about, remained perfectly quiet, after a few spasmodic efforts to escape.

The water shallowed rapidly at this point, and so, getting a line over the saurian's snout, I quickly towed him ashore. It was a long distance to our landing-place, and to tow the alligator across the lake would prove a laborious undertaking. I then concluded to roll him into the boat, and after great labor succeeded in getting his bulky form inside. Then I stepped in myself, and began to paddle shoreward.

Just at this period I noticed with alarm certain signs of resuscitation in the great reptile; first a leg began to quiver, then his uninjured eye twitched, and the great tail began to move about ominously.

By this time I was in deep water, and certainly in a not-to-be-envied position; but I kept on plying the paddle, though the perspiration broke out all over me at the thought of the fix I was in.

There was next a more ferocious gleam in that single eye, a quicker movement of the legs, and the tail came down on the bottom of the boat with a decided whack! I was astride the tail, in the stern, the alligator filling it completely,—for the boat was only twelve feet in length,—and every time that tail came up against the seat I would leap a foot or more, at the same time industriously doing my best to force the boat through the water.

At last the immense head began to move, and the jaws to snap; the tail struck so vigorously against the seat that I thought it would be splintered; still I kept on paddling, with one eye on the 'gator, another on the shore, and

"I WAS ASTRIDE THE TAIL, IN THE STERN OF THE BOAT."

an occasional anxious glance at my gun. If matters came to a crisis, I *could* shoot the 'gator a second time, but it would be at the risk of blowing a hole through the boat at the same time.

Realizing the danger involved in this contingency, I dug desperately at the paddle till my back seemed about to break. I neared the shore; by the vicious look in the 'gator's eye, and the writhing movement throughout his whole body, I saw that he was gathering himself for a last, desperate effort, and that there was no time to lose if I would save my own life.

Realizing this, I threw all my strength into giving impetus to the boat, dropped the paddle, seized my gun, and leaped into the water. How deep it was I did not know till I struck it, but soon discovered that it was up to my arm-pits, though the shore was but a few rods away.

I had left the boat not a second too soon; for into the air flew the seat I was sitting on, and the head and one leg of the alligator were raised over the side. The boat had not lost its impetus, however, and while the 'gator was struggling to get clear, it glided into shallow water and stuck fast on the sand.

At this moment Mr. Alligator overturned it and plunged into the water. "It is my turn now," his whole action seemed to say; and I surely thought it was, for I was even then waist-deep in the water, and my enemy was between me and the shore, though a little to one side. But I had held my gun clear of the water all this time, and there was a charge in the left-hand barrel; had there not been, I hardly know how this episode would have ended.

As the alligator fell clear of the boat, I levelled my gun at his ear-drum and fired. The smoke hid him from sight; but there was a terrific splashing, and although I felt an apprehensive prickling in my legs, I thought the 'gator had received his quietus. And so it proved, when the smoke cleared off; for there he lay, back downward, the white skin of his under parts shining in the sun.

I lost no time in dragging him ashore and in righting the boat, and was glad to find that the splintered thwart was the only damage, besides the wetting, — to which I was used.

After resting awhile I set off for the other 'gator, and an hour later had him stretched beside his brother; two "bull alligators," one measuring nine feet in length, and the other ten.

I skinned them that afternoon, and the vultures came and cleaned the skins next day; and this is the way I secured the hides for my alligator boots.

CHAPTER XVI.

DOWN THE OCKLAWAHA.

IT was midnight, and we were half-way up the stream, — the Hulkwa-wewa ("Bad Water") of the Seminoles, and the Ocklawaha of degenerate "Crackers."

There was rivalry between the two river steamers; the "Okahumkee" passed the "Panasofskee" in the only "reach" wide enough for such a feat, and there was rejoicing and jeering on the one and lamentation and cursing on the other. The bursts of speed were tremendous, at times even reaching the unprecedented rate of four miles an hour. Old steamboat navigators of Florida waters watched this unparalleled attainment with breathless interest, and, whether friend or foe, retired after it was over to drink to an event that "marked the opening of a new era of travel in Florida."

This was at Buffalo Bluff. Victory crowned our efforts; and amid showers of sparks and lurid gleams of light, we passed the "Panasofskee." On the top of our wheelhouse was a blazing fire of pine-knots, which shot its flashes far into the black depths of the swamp. The effect was sublime; tall cypress-trees loomed up like ghosts and waltzed away into the darkness; every lichen on every tree stood out distinct, every tendril of tillandsia, and every seed-pod of the maple. A squirrel, surprised on a limb of a tall tree, dropped his paws in wonderment and stared at us open-mouthed. The last quarter of the old moon shone through the moss-draped limbs of the forest trees; great bunches of mistletoe and clumps of tillandsia, clinging to the blanched tree-trunks, looked like shaggy bears in the white moonlight.

Astern could be seen the red glare of the vanquished "Panasofskee," now gleaming through the trees, now sending a broad lane of light across the stretch of glassy water.

At daylight I climbed to the pilot-house, and found a negro at the helm. What a wonderful descendant of Ham was that negro! How skilfully he guided us, — now shaving a whole broadside of shrubbery, now grazing a protruding stump, and now just slipping over a sunken log! Placid, lake-like reaches, seldom more than a thousand feet in length, gave a bit of variety to the tortuous channel; but nakedness and misery were predominant. Bayous opened out at every turn, dotted with lilies and lettuce, reaching their blue and green into the gray of the cypress. Monarch of the swamp is the cypress, holding high its head and thrusting its spreading feet into the water, about which grow palmettos and interlacing vines. This makes a landing for a little vegetable matter, then a bit of earth, about which gather bignonias and water-lettuce, and land is formed.

The high rate of speed at which we were running required constant feeding of the furnace; and at the first wood yard our steamer stopped, panting and wheezing, and sending valorous puffs through the forest.

Ill-starred "Okahumkee!" Most fortunate "Panasofskee"! This was the opportunity for our rival. She had wood and water; she passed us with triumphant snorts. And she kept ahead. Our superior speed availed us nothing; for attempting to pass her in that narrow channel would be like two trains passing on a single track, — it has been tried, and failed. So we sailed up into Silver Spring, with the "Panasofskee" kicking up her heels at us defiantly, ludicrously, a great cascade breaking and foaming over her stern wheel.

Was this the spring De Leon heard of, this the Fountain of Youth that started him off on his chimerical search? By rare good fortune I have trodden in the footsteps of this gallant old Spaniard, — in Florida, in Guadeloupe, and in Porto Rico, — and everywhere have found that he preferred honor and glory to gold, a peaceful life and its pleasures to the alarms and fatigues of war. He was an exception to the adventurers of those days, — this galliard old hero, this Don Quixote of the New World! It gives an added interest to this beautiful spring to think that the fame of it, as conveyed by the wild Yemassees of the Everglades, should have reached the ears of De Leon, and have thus wrought with the early history of this country one of its most romantic episodes. Description of it at this late day would be a thankless task, as tourists and poets have rhapsodized over it by moonlight and daylight, and poured out their effusions by the ream, by the yard. There are two springs, the larger of which belches forth a volume of water forming a navigable river at the outset. From a ragged cavern sixty feet deep is poured out a flood of clear, sparkling, sulphurous water, so deep that the steamer goes to the very fountain head and hangs poised, as it were, between upper and nether sky; so transparent that the smallest silver coin may be followed by the eye as it sinks to the limestone ledges sixty feet beneath the surface.

To ascend the Ocklawaha by steamer was interesting, though commonplace; to descend it by dug-out would enhance every beauty and add the poetry of exploration to the prose of ordinary travel. A boat was hired, a companion was in readiness, and ere the sun had set on the day of our arrival we were gliding down the stream. For the use of the boat we paid two dollars; she was low, flat, and fifteen feet in length, propelled by paddle-power. The "Okahumkee" was to take her back when we should reach the St. John's, on her return trip. Then of the storekeeper, who had thus honored us with his confidence, we made a purchase for the trip,— a blanket, matches, some fish-lines, crackers, sardines, tin cup, sugar, and eggs. Paddle in hand, we drifted down Silver Spring Run, borne along by a four-mile current past long walls of huge cypress and plots of beautiful lilies, a turn every hundred yards, and every bend revealing some new beauty. Every object on the stream was clearly reflected, and the minutest particle visible on its bed as in the spring itself. Every little while the current was increased by other springs that caused miniature whirlpools above the deep caverns whence they sent out their aqueous tribute.

"Seems like a dream," said my companion, "to be swept so swiftly onward, past such a ceaseless panorama of beautiful scenes."

Five miles down we passed a beautiful orange-grove growing in a deserted clearing; and the Antiquarian clambered ashore, over fallen limbs and drift-logs, and secured a cluster or two of "bitter-sweets." Here the stream was bordered with scarlet cardinal-flowers, wild verbenas, yellow lilies, fragrant nymphæa, and lance-leaved sagittarias.

The Ocklawaha has its source in some small lakes south and west of Silver Spring, though the latter contributes the greatest volume of water. At the confluence of the "run" with the main stream we found a barge, old and abandoned; and here we halted awhile to take a parting glance at the silver stream, which plunged into and was lost in the turbid, sluggish current of the Ocklawaha. Just a hundred miles lay ahead of us before the river joined the St. John's, — a hundred miles through a swamp gloomy and forbidding, with only at long intervals an elevation high enough for a camp at night. The sun was setting as we again entered the boat, turned her head down the stream and to the centre of the sombre channel.

"Over our heads the towering, tenebrous boughs of the cypress
Met in a dusky arch, and trailing mosses in mid-air

Waved like banners that hang on the walls of ancient cathedrals;
Deathlike the silence seemed, and unbroken, save by the herons,
Home to their roosts in the cedar-trees returning at sunset,
Or by the owl, as he greeted the moon with demoniac laughter."

In the gloom we drifted uncertainly. The prospect for a dry camp was not promising, but in turning a bend we saw a light, — an open fire. Near the fire was a woman, over the fire was an iron pot, — both pretty certain evidence that there must be a man near, and hence a shanty and civilization. But this woman advised us not to camp there; she "'lowed" the land was high and dry and the light-wood plenty, but, in her opinion, the water was bad, and would "even spile yer whiskey ef yer had any." The yearning expressed in that woman's face as she interjected this — "ef yer had any" — caused us both to cast an involuntary glance at the blanket covering our "outfit," and then sped us on our way without regret. A mile below we found a place for a camp, landed and made a fire, and, with sardines, tea, and crackers, and a dessert of wild oranges, supped satisfactorily. A pile of palmetto-leaves formed our bed, and here, at our first camp, arose our first dilemma. We had but one blanket. By lying down in that interesting position known as "spoon fashion," we could barely manage to make it cover us. The question arose: Should we sleep on the blanket or under it? should it cover us or we it? This was so perplexing a problem that we sat up half the night trying to solve it. At last it was decided that one of us should sleep outside and the other inside, taking turns at intervals of three hours. We drew lots for position, and it fell to the Antiquarian to take the first outside; but I had not slept half an hour before I awoke shivering with cold, and found my friend rejoicing in a whole "inside," which he had secured by rolling over. After this we slept beneath the blanket, and placed heavy stones at the corners to keep it down. The man with the heaviest ballast on his side generally secured the greater portion of the blanket.

As our fire blazed brightly far into the night, it attracted the attention of some men who had been out hunting limkins, or Indian pullets, and they alarmed us by landing and inspecting the camp. We had but one firearm between us, and that a small revolver, which we both instinctively grabbed for as we awoke and saw those evil-looking faces bending over us. After a social smoke and a pull at the bottle they departed, with little speech, save to warn us against burning too much light-wood from the pile near us, as "the man ez cut that ere light-wood mought bring in a bill afor sun-up." This vision that they had evoked of the watchful wood-cutter filled us with apprehension; and one of us kept hourly watch, in momentary expectation of being prodded with a knife or plugged with a bullet. The stars twinkled, the frogs and lizards chirped, the owls hooted, the limkin sent out his maniac laugh, and the night was vocal with their medley.

The "limkin," or "crying-bird," is such a queer ornithological specimen that I cannot refrain, in this connection, from quoting its quaint description by Bartram. One hundred years ago this enterprising botanist penetrated the then wilderness of Florida, and discovered many things new and strange, among others the limkin. "There is inhabiting the low shores and swamps of this river and the lakes of Florida, a very curious bird, called by an Indian name *Ephouskyca*, which signifies in our language the 'Crying Bird.' It is about the size of a large domestic hen; all the body above and beneath is of a dark lead-color, every feather edged or tipped with white, which makes the bird appear speckled on a near view. The eye is large and placed high on the head; the bill or beak is five or six inches long, arched or bent gradually downward, and flatted at top and beneath, which makes it appear foursquare for more than an inch. The tail is very short, and the middle feather the longest; the two shortest or outermost feathers are perfectly white, which the bird has a faculty of flirting out as quick as lightning, especially when he hears or sees anything that disturbs him, uttering at the same instant an extreme harsh and loud shriek."

This bird uttered its "extreme harsh and loud shriek" all the night through, and thereby much disturbed our rest. At five in the morning we arose from our palmetto couch, cold and stiff, enveloped in a fog that covered river and swamp. The renewing of the fire under these circumstances was a matter of extreme discomfort; but the crackling of twigs and the blazing of pine-knots soon enkindled in us a flame that quickened pulse and limb. To remove the last vestige of fog and chill from our systems, I brewed a pint-cup of egg-nog, — that is what the sinful would call it; but I said it was not regular egg-nog, as it lacked the principal ingredient against which total-abstainers set their faces.

This was Sunday; there arose a question between us, whether we ought to tie up and lie idle all day, or let the boat drift with the current. The Antiquarian advanced the rather specious argument that drifting was not working; that the stream performed its allotted task in obedience to the mandate of a Great Creator, — that it followed on and on, Sabbath and week-day alike; that we might launch our boat and drift upon its bosom without a qualm from even consciences like ours, that had been made tender by New England precepts and case-hardened by repeated applications of Shorter Catechism. "Again," he said, "look at our provisions! a few eggs, a little sugar, and two or three oranges, to say nothing of the low state of our flour and pork!"

His unrighteous argument prevailed. We launched our skiff and drifted with the current. We passed shelly bluffs with understratums of limestone, above which were fields of limited extent containing sheep and bleating lambs. As if further to recall visions of a Northern spring on this January day, we startled, every now and then, great flocks of blackbirds from the corn-like grass, which flew into the trees with whistled "chick-arees;" and a robin, a few warblers, and a wren completed the illusion. The river narrowed, and graceful palms stood up at every point, bignonias and lilies and water-lettuce joining their bases with the water. We drifted through beautiful channels, and looked down long vistas between palmettos and cypress festooned with vines, their images reflected in the mirror-like surface.

Must I pass this dream-land through and by, without securing a more lasting impression than my eye can carry to my senses in this transitory fashion? No! I would photograph its beauties, as I had done at Silver Spring; for a camera and a "dark-tent," containing chemicals and plates, folded into the compass of a large valise, were part of my outfit. But it was the Sabbath!

Again, the ever-ready sinner came to my aid with arguments in favor of improving the time as we went along. "Here were scenes unfolding that we should never look upon again; unless now secured they would be forever lost to us and the world." He prevailed; he had let down the bars at Sunday Bluff; he now drove me into the pasture. The dark-tent was opened and a plate dipped in the silver bath, while the camera was focused in position.

Drawn out from the "bath," the plate was perfectly transparent; it should have been coated with a creamy film. Another was tried, and the bath strengthened, but with like result. In making the collodion my assistant had left out the iodizer. Then my heart sank into my boots, for there was no more collodion nearer than Palatka, one hundred miles away! We packed up and paddled on in gloomy silence. The same thought seemed to be passing through our minds; for suddenly the Antiquarian broke out with, "Well, you didn't break the Sabbath so very much, after all, did you?"

In the afternoon our lesson of the morning was emphasized by our bringing up against a great log fallen across the stream, and by our having to row several miles back to the main channel against the current. A little attention would have prevented this mistake, as that river was as distinctly "blazed" as any path through the forest by the steamboat bumps and bruises on logs and trunks of trees. At one point in this tunnel through the swamp the trees approach so that there is a passage of only twenty-two feet in width, and the steamers have but a foot to spare on either side. This is called the "gate," the gate-posts being two mighty cypresses, their broad buttresses extending deep down into the mud, their ghostly arms and fingers of limbs and branches stretched toward the sky far out of sight, above the overarching canopy of twigs and mosses. Just below the gate is the town and landing of Eureka. What the cracker who opened the place to the world found here when he bestowed upon it the name above, puzzled us to find out. What we found was a landing of stumps, with a plank leading to firmer land beyond. A sagacious man must he have been who bestowed this cognomen upon this landing. He knew of the weakness of the world in general, — to give credit always for what is expressed, without questioning; for, the vision of passing travellers being limited by the barrier of cypress, they would be prone to imagine the unseen land beyond as possessed of charms unutterable.

But I later had cause for imitating the example of the grand old Greek, and joyfully shouting " Eureka ! " at the top of my lungs; for I found here that which enabled us to sail serenely on down the stream, picturing its beauties as we went. A man who met us as we paddled up to the plank at dusk informed us that the owners of the clearing, the " Harrison boys," were absent, but extended an invitation to their cabin. Securing our boat, we followed our new acquaintance to a humble hut of logs, where he made us welcome. The inevitable hog and hominy was our fare, and the floor our bed; but we spread the blanket contentedly, being full of good cheer, with a fire on the hearth before us and a roof above us. At about midnight we heard the tramp of horses' feet, and two brawny men soon after entered, each with a saddle and bridle over his arm, which he flung into a corner. Of course they discovered us lying on their floor, and after the first start drew their housekeeper aside and questioned him. My dark-tent, being the most conspicuous portion of my luggage, excited remark, and one of the new-comers launched at once into a knowing dissertation upon negatives. Hearing this, the Antiquarian nudged me, who required no jogging, for at the first discussion of photographic lore I was awake immediately.

" This feller says," quoth the man who had invited us here, " thet he 's gut tew go to Palatky fer chimmykels; thet he wants tew photygraph the hull river, but his col-colly-something 's give out."

" Collodion 's what you mean, ain't it ? "

" Yis, thet 's it; he 's feelin' kinder pokey about it, 's right smart daown in the mouth. Naow, John, you 've gut some uv thet air, ain't yer ? "

" Yis, I 've gut a bottle on 't somewhar."

" What will you take for it ? "

Their backs were turned toward us, and the conversation had been carried on in a low tone for fear of awaking us. To say that they were surprised at my sudden demand would be stating it but mildly.

"What will you take for that bottle of collodion?"

A satisfactory bargain was concluded, and after much conversation we retired, happy to find, in this isolated clearing, far from any settlement, one of those deluded beings who at some portion of their lives imagine they will wrest a fortune from the world as peripatetic photographers.

The young Harrisons had here a comfortable cabin, ten acres of cleared land, with various outbuildings, a large garden well planted with thrifty orange-trees, and at the river a warehouse and a grist-mill and cotton-gin run by steam. They had taught themselves everything pertaining to the running of the engine and cotton-gin, and seemed to be young men of more than ordinary intelligence. How it warms one's heart to recall,

"TWO BURLY MEN SOON AFTER ENTERED."

even after the lapse of years, such instances of cheerful pluck and large-hearted endeavor as were here manifest! Many a time, when reflecting upon the great number of young men in our cities earning a precarious living by doing woman's work behind counters and in office, have I recalled the noble exertions of these cheerful young men in this clearing in the wilderness. Thousands of acres of land are open to trial in this land of sunshine, which will give a young man decided returns for outlay of labor, in at least refreshing slumber and a contented spirit.

At noon, next day, we drifted down again, through the same tortuous windings, to Log Landing. A picturesque little creek tempted us to make a side exploration, and we rowed past a thrifty little settlement, containing a nursery of orange-trees, cotton and sugar-cane, to where a large water-wheel was slowly revolving; and this made such a pretty picture, with its background of palmettos and cypress, that I tried it with my new collodion with success. The creek had been dammed and furnished sufficient water-power to turn this wheel with its dependent cotton-gins, rice-mill, and grist-mill. In this manner, all over the State, are the citizens of Florida settling the problem of its future.

Running out of the creek into the river, we rowed on, the banks not notably pretty, though hung with an increased abundance of bignonias, past Forty-foot Bluff, — a long, high ridge, crowded with palmettos and deciduous trees. In a couple of hours we suddenly came upon a lone and dilapidated warehouse standing on the river's bank, with a great pile of light-wood and orange-box shooks its only company. This, we concluded, was Iola, where we had been told we should find food and lodging. There was no other sign of house or individual; but after a long walk we reached a rambling, disjointed planter's dwelling, surrounded by fields full of wild plums and cane-grass. In these fields wild rabbits and gophers burrowed in abundance, and flocks of small birds dwelt in the mulberry, oak, and China trees that surrounded the stables and cookhouse. Here we were made welcome, and our goods were locked up in the warehouse.

From this point the famous Orange Lake was at that time reached, and we hired a cart, with mule and attendant driver, to transport us thither, desiring to see a native wild grove in process of being subjected to man. At Ocklawaha Church, a noted landmark, we met the parson on his circuit, which embraced the territory lying between Orange Springs and Silver Springs, twenty-five miles by land, and seventy-five by river. The road was stumpy and sandy, passing through palmetto-scrub and pine-barren, and there were very few settlers. The widow who owned the house at the river had expatiated upon the beauties of the wild grove at Orange Lake in such glowing language that we both had departed from our intended route and gone to the discomfort of this ride of twenty miles in a mule-cart. The grove itself was so far beneath our expectations that we returned three days later in a pet. It was at first proposed to pass the house and go on to the river; but our better feelings prevailed, and we concluded to stop and say good-by. Arrived there, we found the widow departed, but her two demure and pretty daughters in possession and awaiting us with a tempting dinner. Ah! but that was a temptation to stop! But we were thoroughly mad, from our three days of jolting, and steeled our hearts and our stomachs, and turned our faces to the river. The girls seemed grieved that we should slight their hospitable preparations, and I confess to a pang of remorse, even at this day, five years later, that we should have allowed ourselves to be so ungallant. The younger damsel — a black-eyed, tangle-haired beauty of sixteen — did not appear to credit our intentions of leaving, and darted into the garden for some oranges for dessert; and we saw her, as we passed, plucking the golden fruit from the trees.

"Look! did you ever see a lovelier picture?" She stood in the sunlight, with hat hanging loose, clad in pure white, brought into beautiful and strong relief against the dark green of the orange-trees.

"No," replied the unhappy Antiquarian, "I never did; but we can't go back in honor now; let's go on." And so we left the plantation, with many a backward glance and reluctant feet. But we were well punished for our stubbornness that night, by a supperless camp and misfortunes that the sequel will show.

Paddling on, we reached at dusk an overgrown clearing, which, seen through a vista of cypress-trees hung with Spanish moss, and containing a small shanty, invited us to rest there for the night. No man disputed our entry, and we cut fresh leaves for a bed and built a fire near the "lean-to" roof of palmetto-fans. Having now nothing but our tea and a few crackers, we soon had supper disposed of and essayed to sleep. It must have been about midnight — everything of importance always occurs at midnight in a well-conducted camp — that my partner leaped up with a loud shout, and, to my alarmed and sleepy eyes, appeared trying to divest himself of all his apparel.

"I've got a centipede on me, or a scorpion; he's crawling down my back. There! there he is! By Jove, but what a beast!" And he jerked something out from under his vest and flung it on the ground, stamping it out of shape in a second. "Pooh!" said I, "it wasn't anything harmful; there isn't anything of that kind here. Don't you remember what the land-company's books say, — 'There are no noxious insects, not one, in the entire State'?"

"But that was n't an insect, he was too big; he spread himself the whole length of my spine."

"Oh, that's all imagination; you must n't let such little things— Jerusalem! Say, just reach down my back and catch that animal! Oh, I know this is a centipede, sure; he's got a thousand and one legs."

"No, you don't!" retorted the unfeeling Antiquarian; "there are 'no noxious insects' in Florida, hey? How do you like it?"

Meanwhile I was writhing in an agony of apprehension, feeling a most horrible rasping on my skin from this "something" that had crawled down my back. Feeling gingerly for the animal, and with my flesh creeping at the sensation, I at last seized and drew it forth, dropping it at once it was in sight. Then the cause of our terror was revealed as a "walking-stick" insect, with a slender body some four inches long, and wiry legs, looking like an animated green twig. It rolled its protruding eyes so wickedly and felt for us so viciously with its wriggling legs, that, finding a lot more of them in the leaves, we unanimously agreed to sit by the fire the remainder of the night. This we did, groaning over our perverseness at leaving the widow's hospitable roof; and thus the young ladies were avenged.

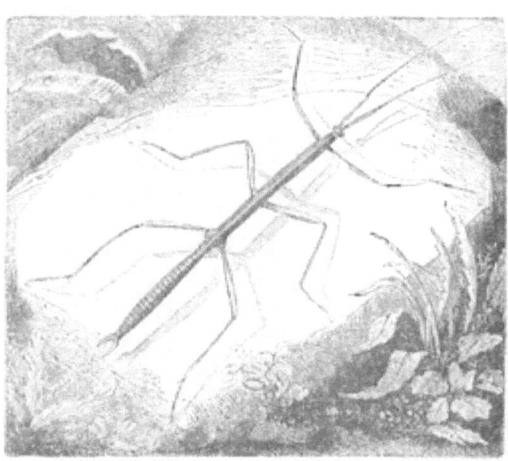

A "WALKING-STICK."

We found a trolling spoon and line tangled in some water-plants, the next morning, probably dragged away from some ascending steamer, and that day we caught some fine black bass. It grieves me to relate that we had no further adventure with the alligator; and though I am aware that the reader will severely frown upon any Florida story without more alligator in it, yet it is impossible to lug one in to this truthful narrative. We saw but few, though every tourist that went up on the steamer and came down on the same, returned boasting that he had slain his thousands and tens of thousands. With our small revolver we peppered at a few black snouts, and once got near enough to one to rap him on the head with a paddle, but captured no more. The river widened, as we neared its embouchure, and approached the mighty St. John's, and we drifted placidly along, past quiet bays and silent creeks that were margined with lily-pads and reflected the woods above them. On the other shore our voyage ended.

University Press: John Wilson & Son, Cambridge.